Early Reading Intervention

Strategies and Methods for Struggling Readers

Catherine Richards
California State University, Long Beach

Jill M. Leafstedt
California State University, Channel Islands

ALLYN & BACON

Boston   New York   San Francisco
Mexico City   Montreal   Toronto   London   Madrid   Munich   Paris
Hong Kong   Singapore   Tokyo   Cape Town   Sydney

Executive Editor and Publisher: *Aurora Martínez Ramos*
Series Editorial Assistant: *Kara Kikel*
Executive Marketing Manager: *Krista Clark*
Production Editor: *Gregory Erb*
Editorial Production Service: *Trinity Publishers Services*

Composition Buyer: *Linda Cox*
Manufacturing Buyer: *Megan Cochran*
Electronic Composition: *Denise Hoffman*
Cover Designer: *Linda Knowles*

For Professional Development resources visit www.allynbaconmerrill.com.

Between the time website information is gathered and then published, it is not unusual for some sites to have closed. Also, the transcription of URLs can result in typographical errors. The publisher would appreciate notification where these errors occur so that they may be corrected in subsequent editions.

Library of Congress Cataloging-in-Publication Data

Richards, Catherine, Professor.
  Early reading intervention : strategies and methods for teaching
struggling readers / Catherine Richards, Jill M. Leafstedt.
      p. cm.
  Includes bibliographical references and index.
  ISBN-13: 978-0-205-57610-4 (pbk.)
  ISBN-10: 0-205-57610-9 (pbk.)
  1. Reading—Remedial teaching.   I. Leafstedt, Jill M.   II. Title.
  LB1050.5.R49 2010
  372.43—dc22

                                    2008045031

Printed in the United States of America

Photo credits: p. 1, Robert Harbison; p. 3, Merrill Education; p. 13, Lindfors Photography; pp. 29, 68, Merrill Education; pp. 38, 75, 147, Lindfors Photography; p. 47, Pearson Learning Photo Studio; p. 71, Lindfors Photography; pp. 91, 111, Ellen Senisi/The Image Works; p. 141, Merrill Education

10 9 8 7 6 5 4 3 2 1   HAM   13 12 11 10 09

Allyn & Bacon
is an imprint of   www.pearsonhighered.com

ISBN-10: 0-205-57610-9
ISBN-13: 978-0-205-57610-4

Contents

We would like to dedicate this book to our mentor and leader of our La Patera team, Michael Gerber. Mike guided us throughout our doctoral training and continues to be an amazing mentor and support. It is with his guidance that we were able to persevere through the many challenges we faced while investigating the Early Reading Project Intervention. Thank you Mike!

Preface

"Before I began intervention, I was sure David was going to have to repeat kindergarten. I just didn't know what to do to get through to him. I thought he was immature. After intervention, I realized he just needed some instruction focused on his individual needs. He is really blossoming."

"Perla is such a great little girl, but when it came to academics, she just wasn't keeping up with the other students. When I tested her, I realized how far behind she truly was. I was then able to design the intervention to meet her needs. She is learning the alphabet and beginning to segment in the phonological awareness activities."

For many students, learning to read is a natural, effortless process; they are exposed to books and literature, taught letters and sounds, and then appear to just begin reading. Others need instruction focused on reading skills and sufficient practice to become successful readers. Still others require specific, intensive instruction to become proficient readers. It is for these students that this book is written. We believe every student can learn to read, but not all students learn to read in the same manner. Some students need more time, more practice, and more specified instruction than others to become readers. These are the students typically labeled "at risk" or "struggling" readers. This group of students must be taught each letter sound, how to blend the sounds together, how to read fluently, and so forth. Therefore, teachers of struggling readers must not just be able to teach reading, they also must know how to teach a struggling reader to read. They must understand the intricacies of the skills needed to learn to read, how to assess them, how to teach them, and how to break them down into simpler parts. In addition, they must do all of this quickly; when working with struggling readers, time is of the essence. Struggling readers are not learning as quickly as their peers and therefore need more practice. Teachers must use effective, efficient strategies to help these students meet their learning goals. The purpose of this book is to provide teachers with the knowledge and skills needed to develop and implement effective, efficient early reading interventions for struggling readers.

Acknowledgments

This book was conceived of on a plane ride home after presenting the Early Reading Project Intervention (ERPI) to a group of teachers in South Carolina. It is for those teachers who asked for something they could take home and share with their colleagues that we wrote this book.

This book would not have been possible if it weren't for the tremendous work of the La Patera research team. This team has grown and changed over the years. Each new formation has added to the knowledge of intervention for young English learners. We would like to thank Terese Aceves, Jessica Cabalo, Judy English, Alexis Filippini, Stacey Kyle, and Emily Solari for the investigations they have conducted that led to the success of the ERPI and made this book possible.

In addition to our colleagues and friends on the La Patera team, we would like to acknowledge Norah Byrom and Susie Keegan. As principal and a teacher at our primary research site, they trusted us with their students and believed that all students could learn to read.

Thanks also go to the reviewers for their valuable feedback: Diana L. Carr, Elgin Junior High School; Amy Cooper, Wilshire Park Elementary School; Freny Dastur, American School of Bombay; Christine Frazer, Henry P. Fieler Elementary School; Tammy Ryan, Jacksonville University; and Renata M. Ziolkowska, California State University, Northridge.

Lastly, we would like to thank our families and friends who supported us through the struggles of writing our first book. Specifically, Jill would like to thank her husband, Mark Haug, who truly believed the book was possible and supported us to the end, her children Tyler and Jeremiah Haug, and her entire family. Cara would like to thank Matthew Tutor for all of his support and love and her parents for always believing in her.

Part One   Foundations

Part One of *Early Reading Intervention: Strategies and Methods for Teaching Struggling Readers* lays out the rationale and research behind the Early Reading Project Intervention (ERPI). Understanding the foundational knowledge presented in Part One is important for teachers in order to implement intervention for struggling readers. Without this knowledge, it is difficult to adapt and modify instruction to meet the needs of individual students who are struggling to read.

We begin in Chapter 1 with an exploration of the development of ERPI, the foundation of ERPI—namely, individual differences in learners—and the differences between ERPI and general classroom instruction. Included is a brief description of the Response to Intervention Model and how the ERPI can be used with this model.

In Chapter 2, we present the five core components of reading, as laid out by the National Reading Panel (2000): phonemic awareness, phonics, fluency, vocabulary, and comprehension. We define the five components and how they relate to the development of reading proficiency. Additionally, Chapter 2 explains the components of early reading—phonological awareness and phonics—and the critical nature of these components in becoming a proficient reader. Chapter 2 is focused on a broad model of reading for struggling readers; in the following two chapters, Chapters 3 and 4, we present the specific needs of English learners and students with learning disabilities.

Chapter 3 provides a focused discussion of the issues related to struggling readers who are English learners (ELs). ELs are a particular focus of this book, because it is often unclear if ELs are struggling to learn to read, struggling to learn English, or both. This chapter provides teachers with the tools to identify struggling readers who are ELs and how to support their overall reading development.

Chapter 4 mirrors Chapter 3, but the focus is on students identified with learning disabilities (LD). This chapter examines differences between struggling readers and readers with learning disabilities and provides a description of how the response-to-intervention model can be used to support both struggling readers and students with learning disabilities. This chapter also provides the instructional methods that are most effective for students with LD and a description of how intervention in early reading skills applies to older students, third through fifth grade, who have not mastered these skills.

Throughout Part One, examples of students who are struggling to learn to read are given. These examples are designed to connect research to classroom practice by presenting real students who are like many of the students we teach.

CHAPTER 1

Basic Concepts

Objectives

By the end of this chapter, the reader will be able to

1. Discuss the Early Reading Project Intervention

2. Explain how the Early Reading Project Intervention relates to response to intervention

3. Describe the difference between intervention and general classroom instruction

This book grew out of extensive research working with kindergarten through second-grade students, many of whom were English learners, as part of two research projects, Project La Patera (Gerber et al., 2004) and the Early Reading Project (Leafstedt, Richards & Gerber, 2004; Richards, Leafstedt & Gerber, 2006). We have titled the intervention the Early Reading Project Intervention (ERPI). The research with the ERPI has shown that direct, explicit, and systematic intervention in early reading skills is effective for improving the phonological awareness skills and the alphabetic principle (phonics) of struggling readers. The ERPI uses a specific teaching method for delivering intervention—the core intervention model (CIM)—which will be discussed in detail in Chapter 6. The ERPI was initially designed and implemented on a large scale, with approximately 400 students who were followed from kindergarten through second grade with positive results (Gerber et al., 2004).

This larger study was followed up with a two-year small-scale study designed to look intensely at 40 kindergarten students as they developed phonological awareness and the alphabetic principle through intervention. This smaller-scale study helped refine both the methods of teaching and the scope and sequence of the intervention. In this study, all of the students but two who participated in the intervention over the two years successfully developed the skills taught. Students responded to intervention in different ways, some learning very quickly, others taking a little more time, and still others needing more ongoing focused instruction to continue growth. During the small-scale implementation of the ERPI, the intervention was modified regularly using data from weekly assessments to meet the individual needs of students as they learned new skills. During this study, the process of development for phonological awareness and the alphabetic principle was studied through ongoing assessment of skills and strategies. The ongoing assessments that were administered were two from the Dynamic Indicators of Basic Early Literacy Skills (DIBELS; details of these assessments will be described in later chapters). Video analysis was used to study student responses during assessment and intervention. This assessment data and video analysis provided the evidence for the scope and sequence of the ERPI, which follows a specific developmental sequence. The various skills and activities in the scope and sequence are designed in a way to meet individual student needs. After many years of research, there is no doubt that when implemented as intended, the ERPI provides struggling readers the boost they need to become proficient in early reading skills and the foundation they need to be successful readers.

Teaching Individuals with Unique Differences

Conducting intervention with homogeneous groups is both effective and efficient for providing intervention. In the ERPI, students were grouped homogeneously, but the **individual differences** that each student within the group possessed were as important, if not even more important, to learning and teaching than the similarities they had with other students in the group. For example, when conducting the ERPI study of 40 kindergarten students, we were working with two students that had very similar profiles. Mario and Juana were both English learners living in extreme poverty. Neither had attended preschool, and both tested similarly low on the initial assessment, which included many different early reading and vocabulary measures. The assessment also showed that the two students had skill deficits in similar areas: phonological awareness skills and letter-sound knowledge. Their classroom teacher was very concerned about both students. Based on the data and teacher observation, the students were placed in the same intervention group.

Intervention lessons were delivered for 10 weeks and followed the scope and sequence of the ERPI. During week 2 of the intervention, it became apparent that the differences these two students had were more important than their similarities. Mario began to learn and learn quickly. He learned each skill and was able to apply his learning to new skills that were taught. Juana, on the other hand, did well during intervention, but each day it was as if the material was brand new. Juana was not mastering the skills. In other words, she could perform the task but did not learn a strategy that allowed her to apply that knowledge to a new task. The individual differences in how the students responded to intervention guided the teacher in designing further lessons. Mario only needed a few more weeks of intervention before he caught up with the other students in the class on early reading skills. After these few weeks, the general reading program was all the support he needed to meet his individual needs in reading. Juana remained in intervention and although successful with the additional help, needed continued support throughout the year. If the individual differences in these students had not been attended to during intervention, Mario and Juana would have received the same instruction and both would have suffered. Mario would have been given intervention for much longer than was necessary, and Juana would have fallen further behind.

Like Juana and Mario, every student, even every struggling reader, is unique. The unique characteristics and individual strengths and needs are part of individual differences. In a class of 25 students, there may be a group of learners who all live in poverty, or a group who all come from two-parent households, or a group that are all learning English as a second language, and likely a group of struggling readers. The struggling readers will form your intervention group. They will have similar areas of need, but the individual differences among the students in how they learn and how they respond to intervention generally will be much larger than their common needs. These individual differences are what guide intervention.

Response to Intervention

Even given the best possible reading instruction, some students will learn to read, and others will struggle. Students respond differently to instruction and may need more and/or different forms of instruction to be successful. In the past, there were not many options for students who struggled with reading, and over time, these students were often referred for special education or retained. However, now there is federal legislation that provides others options for students who struggle and do not respond to instruction.

In 2004, the Individuals with Disabilities Education Improvement Act (IDEIA) was reauthorized to provide an alternative method for how students with learning disabilities are identified. This alternative method, **response to intervention (RTI),** impacts how teachers in both general education and special education support struggling readers. Response to intervention requires that evidence-based reading instruction is provided and that student progress is monitored through ongoing assessments, such as curriculum-based measurements. (Curriculum-based measurement will be described in Chapter 6.) Usually, the Response to Intervention Model has three tiers (Haager, Klinger & Vaughn, 2007; see Table 1.1). Tier 1 instruction is general classroom reading instruction, the core reading program, and involves screening all students to determine those who are at risk. Early in the school year, all students are screened to determine which students are not responding to tier 1 instruction and will need more support. A student who is not responding to instruction at tier 1 is provided more intensive reading intervention than at tier 2. Interventions in tier 2 are short-term explicit interventions, and students are assessed regularly to determine if they are making progress with the intervention. Each school and district decides how to provide the intensive intervention and who will provide it. Some schools may choose to continue intervention in the general education classroom while also differentiating instruction in small groups. Others may employ reading specialists who work with students; still others may use special education teachers to provide intervention. With more intensive intervention at tier 2, some students will respond to intervention and make the progress necessary to catch up with their peers. For these students, intervention can be discontinued. However, there will likely be some students for whom tier 2 intervention is not enough; these students who are not responsive will need tier 3 intervention. Tier 3 is an even more intensive level of reading intervention, and students who need this level of support in reading may be considered for special education under the category of learning disabilities. As with tiers 1 and 2, progress is monitored regularly, often weekly, in tier 3 to determine if the student is making progress and/or if instructional changes need to be made. See Table 1.1 for an overview of the three-tier model.

Traditionally, students have been identified as having a learning disability by a discrepancy between their score on an IQ measure and an achievement measure (Stuebing et al., 2002). That is, students with learning disabilities are those students who have average intelligence as measured by IQ and a below average achievement that is unexpected. Generally, these students are not identified until third grade or later and therefore are not provided services until they have fallen far

TABLE 1.1 **Overview of the Three Tiers of the Response to Intervention Model**

Tier	Instruction	Assessments
Tier 1	Research-based reading curriculum being implemented with fidelity by general education teachers	Screening assessments given 3 or 4 times a year
Tier 2	Intensive, explicit intervention for a specified period of time (3 to 5 days a week, 30 minutes per day for 10 to 12 weeks) provided by a general education teacher or other personnel	Weekly, biweekly, or monthly progress monitoring (CBM) during intervention
Tier 3	More intensive, sustained intervention and possibly special education services	Weekly or biweekly progress monitoring

behind their peers (MacMillan & Siperstein, 2002). RTI allows schools to identify struggling students and provide students intervention early on in kindergarten and in first and second grade (Vaughn, Wanzek, Woodruff & Linan-Thompson, 2007). Under an RTI model, students are provided the interventions they need early in order to prevent reading failure and possibly the need for special education services.

The Early Reading Project Intervention (ERPI) is a research-based intervention that can be used to prevent later reading failure. The ERPI is aligned with tier 2 interventions in the RTI model, and it also can be intensified to meet the needs of students in tier 3 intervention. In Part Two of this book, we provide the content and methods that can be adapted for both tiers.

Intervention versus General Classroom Instruction

It is not uncommon in a typical intervention program for students to review and repeat the work done during general classroom reading instruction. However, reading intervention should be different from even the best general classroom reading instruction. General classroom reading instruction is provided to all students and designed to meet the needs of the majority of students in a class. However, reading intervention is not necessary for all students and is only provided to those

who need it. It is designed to meet the specific needs of students for whom general classroom instruction is not enough. Typically, 20 to 30 percent of the students in a class will need instruction in addition to the standard reading curriculum (Vaughn & Roberts, 2007; Vaughn et al., 2007). This book provides teachers with a guide for designing **interventions,** specifically using the content and methods of the ERPI, to supplement general instruction for students in need of early reading intervention.

Both intervention and general classroom reading instruction should use methods that have proven effective through research and

TABLE 1.2 Comparison of Reading Instruction and Reading Intervention

Reading Instruction	Reading Intervention
• Is evidence based	• Is evidence based
• Includes 5 components of reading	• Includes 5 components of reading
• Uses multiple teaching methods	• Targets specific skill deficits
• Meets the needs of the whole group	• Uses systematic, explicit, and direct methods
• Generally is not based on mastery	• Meets the need of individual students
	• Is based on mastery learning

classroom practice. However, there are differences between general classroom reading instruction and reading intervention (see Table 1.2). Strong reading instruction is based on multiple teaching methods that address the multiple components of reading both in isolation and in combination. Such instruction also meets the needs of a heterogeneous population of students. General classroom reading instruction is often organized around a spiral curriculum, in which ideas and skills are taught and revisited throughout the year (Bruner, 1960). Students are not expected to master a skill at any specific time during the year, because there is the expectation that the skill will be reintroduced and expanded on later in the year. Intervention, on the other hand, is designed to focus on small groups of students with similar learning needs; it is focused on clear objectives and is short in duration, usually 20 to 30 minutes a day for 8 to 12 weeks. Intervention insists on mastery learning, in which a skill is taught until the student has become proficient. Intervention is also explicit, meaning that the teacher and students know the objectives and that each skill is taught directly by the teacher, with opportunities for students to practice. Intervention instruction must also be systematic, following a specific sequence of skills that build on each other.

In a classroom where intervention is taking place, you will see about four students sitting close to the teacher; the students will be responding quickly and often; the goals and objectives will be clear to any trained observer; teacher talk will be minimized and focused; student rate of response will be high; and students will be regularly praised for correct answers. Teachers will often use hand gestures instead of words to indicate to students it is their turn to respond. General classroom reading instruction looks different and can vary greatly from class to class. Typically, students are in a whole group for introduction of the material, have some review in a small group, and then have time to work independently. The goals and objectives tend to be broader and are based on state standards, not individual students' abilities. Typically, the written goals and objectives do not take into account the diversity of individuals in any given classroom. Unlike intervention, most general reading instruction will move forward even if students have not mastered the skills. The distinction between instruction and intervention is important to understand, because intervention is not just more of the same instruction given at a different time of day or with a smaller group of students. Intervention looks, sounds, and is different than typical classroom instruction. General classroom reading instruction is designed to meet the needs of the majority of students in the class. Intervention, on the other hand, should support classroom instruction but is designed around the needs of individual students.

Summary

The Early Reading Project Intervention (ERPI) has been designed based on extensive research examining the effects of the intervention on early reading skills, specifically phonological awareness and the alphabetic principle. The ERPI has a focus on individual learners and the individual differences they possess rather than the similarities that bring them together in a teaching group. Not all students will need intervention, but for those readers who do need intervention, explicit, systematic intervention that supports but is different from general reading instruction should be provided. The ERPI is designed as an intervention for students who need more than tier 1 general classroom instruction—that is, either tier 2 or tier 3 interventions.

CHAPTER 2

Overview of Reading Intervention

Objectives

By the end of this chapter, the reader will be able to

1. Describe the five core components of reading: phonological awareness, phonics, fluency, vocabulary, and comprehension

2. Describe the relationship between the five core components of reading

3. State why phonological awareness and phonics are critical to include in early reading intervention

Learning to read is a complex process. This process occurs quite easily for some and is challenging for others. This chapter provides an overview of the complex process of learning how to read and describes the research that supports the use of early reading intervention to reduce reading difficulties. To conduct effective reading intervention, it is critical to determine the individual needs of students. In order to determine individual student needs, teachers need to understand how students learn to read and the essential skills required in the process of learning to read.

There is and likely will always be much debate about how students become successful readers. Researchers and teachers continue to debate whether directly teaching reading is more or less effective than allowing students to acquire reading skills through experiences, exposure, and other less direct methods. From the authors' perspective, this debate lies within the individual student. In other words, the individual differences students possess impact how they learn to read and how much instruction is needed for them to become proficient readers. To illustrate individual differences in learning to read, we provide two case examples, Scott and Erin.

Scott is a third-grader who cannot keep his nose out of a book. He reads at the sixth-grade level and loves reading Harry Potter books. Often his teacher gets frustrated because Scott rushes through other work just to get a chance to have free reading time. Scott went to a year of preschool, but even before preschool, he would make up silly rhymes and "spell" (using invented spelling) words on the refrigerator with magnetic letters. When he got to kindergarten and was introduced to letter-sound correspondences and some basic sight words, he could read. His mom and dad were surprised and so was his teacher. It seemed as if one day he could just all of a sudden read. He quickly read through all of the kindergarten-level books and moved on to first-grade-level books by the middle of kindergarten. He could tell you everything about what he read and how the story or topic related to his own life and experiences. At times, he came to a word he was not sure about and would ask the teacher. She would tell him, "Sound it out and then read it so it makes sense." He would and was usually able to figure the word out. Scott was being exposed to general reading instruction through whole class instruction that included the five core reading components: phonological awareness, phonics, fluency, vocabulary, and comprehension. Scott did not receive explicit, systematic reading instruction in each of the components, but he never needed it. Most of us have seen a handful of children like Scott over our years of teaching. For these students—who really learn to read without much help from us—we, as teachers, are their guides in learning, providing them books and other materials, exposing them to various types of text and topics, and keeping them motivated to read and learn new concepts.

On the other hand, there are students who learn because of our teaching. They do not naturally learn to read. Erin, also a third-grade student, struggles every day to keep up with her peers and works very hard. Erin went to preschool for two years and was able to do rhyming activities with the whole class. She listened intently to the stories read by her teacher. She loved drawing pictures about the stories after hearing them. Her parents would read stories to her at home, and she would talk about the stories with them after they were read. When she got to kindergarten, she knew all the letters in her name, but by the middle of the year, she had not learned all the letters and sounds that had been taught. She also really struggled with segmenting sounds in words, a skill that many of the other students in her class could do at that point in the year. Luckily, Erin's kindergarten teacher used a reading program that provided systematic and explicit instruction early on in the year. By first grade, Erin had learned all her letters and sounds and was segmenting and blending words orally. However, she was now struggling with decoding basic words. Her first-grade teacher also used a reading program that provided explicit and systematic instruction in early reading skills and provided Erin supplemental intervention in basic decoding skills. By the end of first grade, Erin was on track with her peers. The explicit and systematic instruction provided by her kindergarten and first-grade teachers gave her the extra help she needed to read at grade level. Now in the third grade, her teacher monitors Erin closely and continues to provide her very explicit instruction with multiple opportunities to practice and review skills and concepts. By providing Erin the explicit, systematic instruction she needed, her teachers have been instrumental in her learning to read. Erin would not have learned to read without this type of instruction.

When determining the type of instruction to provide struggling readers like Erin, the debate on how to teach reading becomes different (Kavale & Forness, 1987; Lloyd, 1984). Decades of research support explicit and systematic reading instruction aimed at the needs of individual struggling readers. Research has demonstrated that struggling readers need to be directly taught reading skills and taught how to put these skills together to read successfully (Adams, 1990; Chall, 1967, 1983; Engelman & Carnine, 1982). Although there is much debate about how all students learn to read, it is quite clear that students who are struggling to learn to read have the best outcomes when they are provided explicit, systematic instruction.

The National Reading Panel's Approach to Reading

The first step in providing explicit, systematic reading instruction is to understand what needs to be taught. When teachers understand how students learn to read, it is much easier to identify and directly teach skills to meet individual student needs. Reading is a process that is made up of core components that can be taught and assessed to improve student outcomes. The Early Reading Project Intervention (ERPI) presented in this book is based on findings from the National Reading Panel (NRP). In 1997, the NRP was convened to review existing approaches to teaching reading. Among the findings, the panel concluded that systematic early reading instruction is imperative for struggling readers. This instruction should be based on five core components: phonemic awareness, phonics, fluency, vocabulary, and comprehension. Years of research, synthesized by the NRP panel, has demonstrated that teaching the five components of reading enables students to become successful readers. Each of these five components is defined and described in Table 2.1.

**TABLE 2.1   The National Reading Panel's
Five Components of Reading**

Component	Definition
Phonemic awareness	"Phonemic awareness refers to the ability to focus on and manipulate phonemes [individual sounds] in spoken words" (NRP, 2000, p. 2-1). An example of a phonemic awareness skill is the ability to segment sounds in a word (i.e., *cat* is /c/a/t/). Phonemic awareness is one of the earliest reading skills to develop.
Phonics	Phonics skills include knowing letter-sound correspondences and applying them to reading and spelling (NRP, 2000) This is sometimes termed the alphabetic principle. Phonics skills begin developing as students are introduced to the alphabet and sounds and continue to develop until students are proficient readers.
Fluency	Fluency is the ability to read quickly and accurately. A student who is a fluent reader also reads with expression. Fluency develops after students have sufficient phonics skills to be able to decode words accurately. Fluency continues to improve as students gain more knowledge of phonics and build their vocabulary (NRP, 2000).
Vocabulary	Vocabulary is the understanding of the meaning of individual words, both orally and when reading (NRP, 2000). Vocabulary begins developing in very young children well before they begin school and impacts understanding of written words as they begin to read.
Comprehension	Comprehension is the ability to make meaning of text (NRP, 2000) and includes several subskills, including, but not limited to, the four skills listed above. Comprehension skills develop early, initially in the form of listening comprehension as books are read aloud to students. Later, students must piece together these various components of reading to both read and to understand their reading.

Relevance of Each Component

Each of the five components is individually important in the process of learning to read. Each component is also intricately related to the others. In fact, these skills are so closely related to one another that it is often difficult to distinguish when a student is struggling in one area and not others. Many nonstruggling students learn the five components in an interrelated manner. It may not be necessary for these students to learn each component separately. Struggling readers, however, need teachers to understand the details of the reading process because they need to be taught each of the components explicitly and often independently of the others. Struggling readers also need to be directly taught the relationship among the components and how, together, they are used to read successfully.

The first component in the NRP model is phonemic awareness. **Phonemic awareness** is the ability to hear individual sounds, or phonemes, in words and includes blending, segmenting, and manipulating these individual sounds. In this book, the broader term **phonological awareness** (PA) is used to include other subskills such as rhyming, identifying beginning sounds, and segmenting onset-rime portions of words. PA is a purely auditory skill that begins developing at a very young age before children even know letter names and corresponding sounds. PA is a cornerstone in early reading interventions. Without PA, most likely a student will struggle with learning to read.

Decades of research demonstrate that the lack of PA is an accurate predictor of later reading difficulties (NRP, 2000; Wagner, Torgeson & Rashotte, 1994; Wagner et al., 1997). PA is strongly related to students' current word reading (Jongejan, Verhoven & Siegel, 2007) and future word reading abilities (Schatschneider et al., 2004). That is, a student who has strong PA skills in kindergarten will likely read some basic words in kindergarten and be reading many words by first grade. The reverse is also true. For example, Eddie, a kindergarten student, is not able to identify rhyming words or segment words into individual sounds. Because of these PA skill deficits, we know that Eddie will be at risk for word reading difficulty in first grade. Without extra support and intervention in PA, his word-reading difficulties will continue and greatly impact his later fluency and comprehension abilities.

For educators who work with struggling readers like Eddie, the good news is that PA can be taught and thus act to prevent later reading difficulties (Ehri et al., 2001; Foorman et al., 1997; Torgesen,

Wagner & Rashotte, 1999). This same research also indicates that for many students, about 300 minutes of instruction, which is about 30 minutes a week (10 minutes, three days a week) for 10 weeks is adequate for students to make gains in PA skills. When PA interventions are provided intensively (30 or more minutes each day), approximately 94 to 98 percent of students with reading difficulties will learn PA skills and go on to become proficient word readers (Torgesen, 2000). This means that if a first-grade teacher has a class of 20 students and provides explicit, systematic instruction in PA to all students and intervention in PA to struggling students, then all but about one student will become a strong word-level reader.

When teaching PA to a student like Eddie, teachers should follow a specific instructional sequence, since PA is a developmental skill that is learned in a predictable manner (Christensen, 1997; Leafstedt, 2003; Chiappe, Siegel & Gottardo, 2002). The first indicator that students are developing PA is their ability to identify beginning sounds and rhyming sounds in words. Initially, students can tell if words start with the same beginning sounds or rhyme. Soon they can segment the initial sound from the rime portion of the word (see Chapter 5). For example, a student will tell that the sounds in *cat* are /c/-/at/. When students are near mastery of this skill, they begin to segment all the sounds in words and blend sounds together to make a word. This ability to segment and blend individual sounds in words is critical to early reading (NRP, 2000). For example a student who can hear individual sounds in *cat*—/c/-/a/-/t/—is more likely to sound out the individual sounds in written words and blend the sounds back together to read the word.

The second component of the NRP model of reading instruction is phonics. **Phonics instruction** is a way to teach students the **alphabetic principle**. The alphabetic principle involves understanding how written letters and sounds are connected (NRP, 2000). The alphabetic principle includes several subskills: letter-sound knowledge, sounding out words (**decoding**), and reading connected text (Simmons & Kame'enui, 1998). By becoming proficient with the alphabetic principle, students can focus on reading fluently and comprehending what they have read. Phonics instruction provides students with the skills they need to quickly and easily decode new words they encounter while reading.

Phonics instruction typically begins in kindergarten with basic letter-sound correspondence and decoding consonant-vowel-consonant (CVC) words. The instruction quickly becomes more complex in first

and second grade, including decoding words with letter combinations, such as blends and digraphs, and multisyllabic words. Research indicates that explicit, systematic phonics instruction is highly effective (NRP, 2000; Engelmann & Carnine, 1982). When phonics is not taught explicitly, many students will struggle with comprehension, either in the early grades or as they progress through school, since the text language becomes more complex, requiring the ability to decode many new words (NRP, 2000).

Research shows that phonics instruction should be systematic and follow a prescribed sequence of instruction (NRP, 2000). Phonics instruction that is not systematic and is developed only as needed by the teacher has not been found to be as effective. In a reanalysis of the NRP report, Hammill and Swanson (2006) agreed that systematic phonics instruction is important particularly for young at risk students, even though their findings indicated that the effects of this instruction were smaller than originally reported by the NRP.

Explicit, systematic phonics instruction has been shown to be especially important for students from families with low socioeconomic status (Engelmann, 1999; Engelmann, Becker, Carnine & Gersten, 1988). A large study, *Follow Through* (Engelmann et al., 1988), that began in the 1960s and continued until the 1980s, showed that students in the primary grades from disadvantaged backgrounds performed better in reading when provided reading instruction focused on systematic phonics using direct instruction methods, specifically the DISTAR program. Students who received the DISTAR program performed better than students who received other instructional programs. Since then, several studies examining the impact of systematic phonics using direct instruction have been conducted and show similar results indicating the benefit of this approach to phonics instruction for students in general education and special education (Adams & Engelmann, 1996; Adams & Carnine, 2003).

Fluency, the third component of the NRP reading model, is the ability to read connected text quickly and accurately. Fluent readers are able to better understand what is being read because they are able to focus on meaning and not individual words. Let's look at another student, Robert, as an example. Robert reads slowly and painfully sounds out each word when he reads text. Although he correctly decodes each word, even difficult words that have blends and digraphs and are multisyllabic words, he cannot recall what he has read. Robert is not fluent in reading because he is still focusing on reading individual words. Robert needs to practice reading and rereading connected text so he can become fluent and gain meaning from what he reads. When students must decode each word, they are not able to understand the meaning of the text as a whole, although they may comprehend individual words in isolation. This problem occurs because they are using all their **working memory** to process the word so they do not have enough **cognitive capacity** to understand what has been read. Most people can hold about seven items in their working memory (Baddley & Hitch, 1974). If those items are individual sounds, there is not enough room for the words or phrases that allow for meaning to be processed.

Vocabulary, the fourth component in the NRP model of reading, is a complex skill. It both impacts and is impacted by reading. In other words, students who have a large vocabulary will use their vocabulary to decode words and make sense of what they read. Likewise, students who are fluent readers will build their vocabulary more quickly by reading (Juel, Biancarosa, Cocker & Deffes, 2003; Biemiller & Slonim 2001). Additionally, it is known that vocabulary is highly related to a family's socioeconomic status (Graves, Brunetti & Slater, 1982; White, Graves & Slater, 1990). Children from upper-class families know twice as many words as children from families who are on welfare (Hart & Risley, 1995, 2003). This difference in vocabulary grows more discrepant over time between these two groups of students (Biemiller, 2003; Stanovich, 1986) and can greatly impact students' overall reading abilities.

Vocabulary knowledge is an ongoing and continuously developing skill and is an essential part of reading instruction. For students who are struggling to learn to read, it is important to directly teach vocabulary. Teaching vocabulary aids in comprehension of text (NRP, 2000). A successful reader can learn vocabulary indirectly through exposure or experience in reading or in books read aloud. However, struggling readers are less likely to learn new words from independent reading (Nagy, Herman & Anderson, 1985) or by listening to stories read aloud (Robbins & Ehri, 1994). These students need to be directly taught the vocabulary words in order to comprehend what is being read. Teachers must systematically select words that are related to specific stories or content text and common words that are likely to be encountered in various stories or content text (Beck, McKowen & Kucan, 2002).

For struggling students, extended, explicit instruction in vocabulary may be needed and has been demonstrated to be effective (Coyne, Kame'enui & Simmons, 2004; Coyne, McCoach & Kapp, 2007; Penno Wilkinson & Moore, 2002).

For young students who are struggling to learn to read, most opportunities for developing vocabulary are through books read aloud. During a "read aloud," the teacher should directly teach important vocabulary. During reading intervention, in which students are learning PA and phonics skills and working on gaining fluency, the books that students will read have controlled vocabulary to facilitate independent reading (Carnine, Silbert, Kame'enui & Tarver, 2004; Hiebert, Martin & Menon, 2005). Books with controlled vocabulary are perfect for teaching word reading and fluency. However, these books do not contain sufficient diversity in words to build a student's vocabulary; therefore, teachers should have an array of literature books for developing critical vocabulary needed to facilitate comprehension.

Comprehension is the culminating component included in the NRP model of reading. Comprehension is the ultimate goal of reading and is a complex process that involves each of the above four components as well as comprehension strategies to make meaning of text. Research in the area of text comprehension indicates that the direct teaching of comprehension strategies improves understanding of text and facilitates independent learning (NRP, 2000). Students who show difficulties in comprehending text may struggle with decoding and fluency, may have difficulty with vocabulary, may not have learned efficient comprehension strategies, or may have deficits in all three of these areas. Three case examples are presented below that illustrate each of these potential reasons for not comprehending written text. Within each case study are instructional implications for addressing the comprehension difficulties.

Ms. Kramer, a third-grade teacher, has many students in her class who struggle with comprehending expository text. For this reason, she decided to teach her class two comprehension strategies for expository text: extracting the main idea and summarizing critical information using a graphic organizer. She is most concerned about three students in her class—Aryanna, Christopher, and Andy—who are failing science and social studies. All three appear to be good students who listen and participate. However, their independent work is very poor. Ms. Kramer decides that these three students would benefit from small

group instruction that focuses on these comprehension strategies. She decides to begin with science material first. After a few weeks, Ms. Kramer notices that Christopher has really benefited from the additional instruction, and she has seen his science work improve. She has not seen the same the impact on his social studies work. Ms. Kramer decides that she will teach a couple of lessons using social studies content to help Christopher generalize these strategies.

Unlike Christopher, Aryanna and Andy do not seem to be benefiting from the additional instruction. Even though during small group instruction they both have been able to apply the strategies, Ms. Kramer does not see a change in their work. Often, teachers of students in the upper elementary grades observe a student who is having comprehension difficulties and aim to teach the student comprehension strategies. However, at times, comprehension is not the skill the student needs to be taught. Ms. Kramer decides to work with Aryanna and Andy one on one to see if she can discover more information. After working with Andy, Ms. Kramer realizes that when reading the text, he can read quite fluently but does not know the meaning of many common academic words (e.g., *compare, issue, predict, determine,* etc.). Ms. Kramer decides that Andy needs very explicit instruction in these vocabulary words that are common in many expository texts.

When Ms. Kramer has Aryanna read aloud, she struggles to decode at least one or two words in each sentence. These struggles inhibit her fluency and also her comprehension of the material. On the surface, Aryanna appears to be a decent reader, but when presented with novel words, she is not a fluent reader. Ms. Kramer decides to assess Aryanna's reading skills to get a clear picture of the skills she is lacking. After assessing, Ms. Kramer plans to conduct an intervention focused on decoding multisyllabic words and fluency with grade-level text.

For students at any grade level, all other reading components need to be developed for students to comprehend what they are reading. Comprehension is a difficult skill to teach because it is complex and multifaceted. For Christopher, extra instruction in comprehension strategies was exactly what he needed to begin to gain meaning from the texts. However, for Andy and Aryanna, other skill deficits were contributing to their comprehension problems. If a student's comprehension problems are due to vocabulary issues like Andy's, words should be taught directly so that a student can build the necessary vocabulary to understand what is being read. If a student's comprehension difficulties are due to difficulty in the area of phonics and/or fluency, these skills should be taught first to see if by improving these skills comprehension also improves. If a student like Aryanna struggles with phonics and fluency, then teaching complex comprehension skills will not necessarily lead to improved comprehension. Once Aryanna develops fluency with text, then her comprehension may also improve. However, she may still need instruction in specific comprehension skills, since not all students who can decode and read fluently will comprehend.

Relationship among the Components

Each of the five components of reading is necessary but not sufficient for students to become proficient readers. Students must not only apply each individual skill, they also must integrate the skills. Furthermore, each component relates to a student's ability to learn the other components (see Figure 2.1). If students do not have phonological awareness, they will have difficulty learning to decode words and will struggle with

FIGURE 2.1   Relationship among the Five Components of Reading

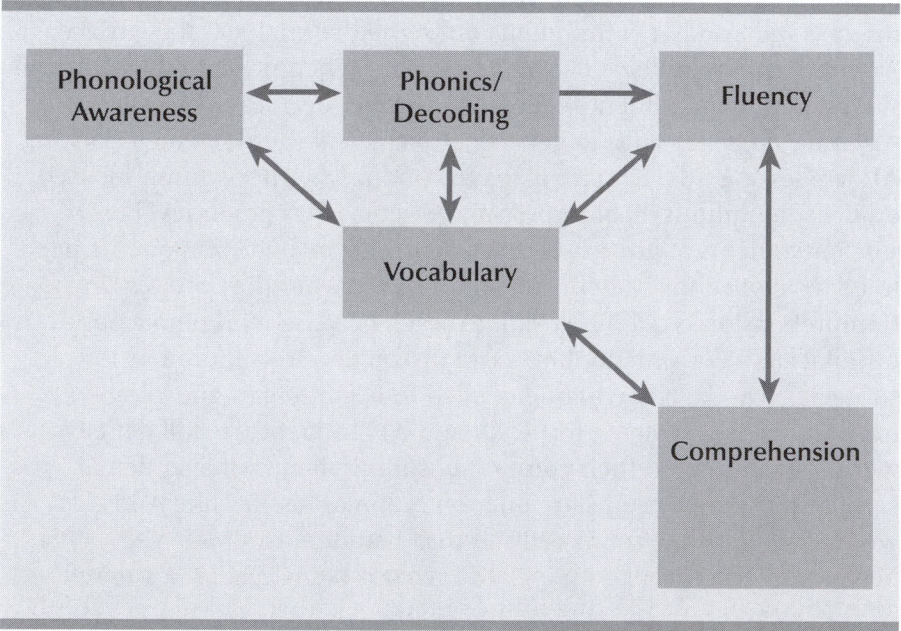

phonics. Without the ability to hear the sounds in words, it will be difficult for a student to develop sound-symbol relationships and decoding words. Decoding is the ability to use letter-sound knowledge to break up sounds in words and then blend those sounds back together. It is logical, then, that if students have a hard time decoding individual words, they will not be fluent readers. If students spend a great deal of time sounding out individual words, students will not have the cognitive capacity to read fluently. Fluent reading leads to stronger comprehension. There is a strong correlation between oral reading fluency and reading comprehension (National Assessment of Educational Progress, 2002). Therefore, most students who can read fluently have strong comprehension skills (Snow, Burns & Griffith, 1998; NRP, 2000). Despite this relationship between fluency and comprehension, students with limited vocabulary may be able to read fluently and still not understand what they have read. This can be an issue for English learners. (See Chapter 3.)

Vocabulary knowledge is complex. It plays a dual role in reading: it helps a student become a better reader, and it is improved through reading. For example, if Robert is trying to decode a word that he has in his oral vocabulary, it will be easier for him to decode the word in a text than if he did not have the word in his vocabulary. Likewise, if a student has strong reading skills and encounters a novel word, it will be easier for him or her to learn the meaning of that word by using context clues. The larger the student's vocabulary, the easier it is for the student to read and understand what has been read. Therefore, the more a student reads, the greater the student's vocabulary will be.

Comprehension encompasses phonological awareness, phonics, fluency, and vocabulary. In addition, it includes individual text comprehension skills and strategies (i.e., main idea, inferencing, visualizing, self-monitoring). A difficulty in any one of these components can lead to comprehension problems. On the other hand, if all of these pieces are in place, a student is on the way to becoming a proficient reader (NRP, 2000)

Early Reading

Early reading is defined, for purposes of this book, as the components of reading that develop early in the process of learning to read. All components develop throughout a student's schooling, but a few of the components develop earlier and must be present for the other components to work effectively and efficiently. The two components most often considered to be part of early reading are phonological awareness (PA) and phonics. When PA and phonics are developed, students are prepared to decode individual words and begin reading with fluency. If students do not have a solid foundation in these skills as they move into the upper grades, they will consistently struggle when encountering new words. This is not to say that the other components of reading are not important or should be ignored. For example, vocabulary and comprehension should be directly taught during general classroom reading instruction so that students are exposed to the meaning of new words and begin to develop strategies for comprehension. However, for struggling readers, intervention in addition to general classroom reading instruction in PA and phonics can eliminate many later reading problems. In fact, research has shown that all but 2 to 6 percent of struggling readers who participate in early reading interventions can become proficient readers (Torgesen, 2000). When students do not master PA and phonics in the early grades, these difficulties cause them to fall farther and farther behind their peers.

Figure 2.2 shows that students who were below the benchmark goal in early reading at beginning of first grade never caught up with their peers who met the benchmark in first grade. Furthermore, the gap between these students and those that did meet the benchmark widens as the students progress through school. This demonstrates that the early reading skills are foundational skills and that they must be developed for students to become successful readers.

Early reading skills include PA and phonics and, as students are ready, reading connected text. Generally speaking, early reading skills should be focused on during preschool until second grade. Students who acquire these skills as early readers are more likely to have strong word-level reading skills and therefore strong comprehension. By the second grade, the curriculum begins to focus on comprehension, and students are expected to begin learning from what they read. Less attention is focused on the actual task of learning how to read. Ideally, teachers will want to intervene with a student who is struggling in PA and phonics in kindergarten or first grade. If students have not acquired these early reading skills by second grade, extremely intensive intervention is needed.

**FIGURE 2.2   Trajectory of Growth for First-Grade
Oral Reading Fluency**

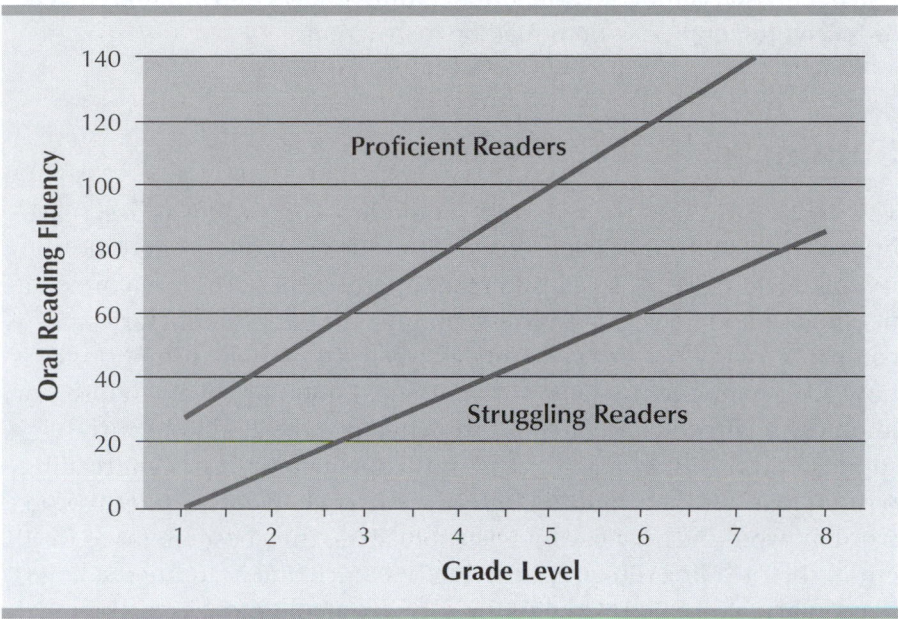

Early Reading Intervention versus
Early Reading Classroom Instruction

As discussed in Chapter 1, this book is about intervention that is conducted in addition to general classroom reading instruction. When teaching the components of reading, general classroom instruction will look very different than intervention. When teaching reading to all students, whole group instruction focuses on multiple components within one lesson. For instance, students may be presented with a story or a chapter for the week and then learn a new sound or sounds to decode while working to improve their fluency. At the same time, they may be exposed to new vocabulary words associated with the story and expected to answer comprehension questions or do a writing activity related to the story. Intervention, on the other hand, is conducted in a small group and targeted on specific objectives based on individual student needs. Students should participate in intervention until they have mastered the skills that they are lacking. When students have reached mastery, they no longer need intervention and will only need to receive general classroom reading instruction.

Summary

This chapter outlines the five core components of reading as described by the NRP (2000). Proficiency in each of the components and the ability to integrate the skills leads to reading proficiency. The five core components—phonological awareness, phonics, fluency, vocabulary, and comprehension—are defined and described. Of particular importance is how each component relates to the others. Phonological awareness and phonics are intricately related, as students must be able to hear the sounds in words in order to sound out words when they begin reading written text. When beginning to read, or decode, words, students read word by word. As they become better readers, they become more fluent in their reading. Fluency is defined as quick and accurate reading. Vocabulary, although related to the other components, has a reciprocal relationship with reading. The more a student reads, the larger the student's vocabulary. Likewise, the larger a student's vocabulary, the easier it is for the student to read. Comprehension, the final component, is dependent on the other four components being sufficiently developed. If students have areas of need in any of the other four areas, their ability to comprehend text will be compromised.

Each of the five core components is important in reading, but only two are considered early reading skills for the ERPI—phonological awareness (PA) and phonics. PA and phonics are both skills that can be taught, with positive effects, to struggling readers. When PA and phonics intervention are conducted for struggling readers, the great majority of these students will go on to become proficient in word reading. This proficiency will provide them with a stepping-stone to fluency and comprehension.

CHAPTER 3

Providing Reading Intervention to English Learners

Terese C. Aceves and Michelle P. Windmueller

Objectives

By the end of this chapter, the reader will be able to

1. Describe the characteristics of English learners, including the heterogeneity among this group of students

2. Differentiate student characteristics that relate to second language acquisition and those that relate to a learning disability

3. Describe an intervention designed to meet the unique needs of English learners

One of the major challenges currently facing our educational system is that of providing appropriate instruction to increasing numbers of students from various cultural and linguistic backgrounds. According to the Urban Institute, the number of school-age children of immigrant parents grew from 6 percent in 1970 to 19 percent in 2000 (VanHook & Fix, 2000). By 2004, approximately 9.9 million school-age children spoke a language other than English in the home. Many of these learners experience great difficulty keeping up with increasing standards-based instructional practices and high-stakes testing requirements brought about by district, state, and federal mandates. Under these conditions, English learners (ELs) often demonstrate lower academic achievement, higher grade repetition, and a higher incidence of school dropout in comparison to monolingual English peers (Abedi, 2002; August & Hakuta, 1997). Could these negative outcomes for ELs result from inadequate instruction, low levels of English language proficiency, general learning problems, or other contributing factors?

These poor academic outcomes may result from differences between home and school environments and/or bias in the referral and assessment process for disability identification and may contribute to the over- and sometimes underidentification of ELs for special education programs (Donovan & Cross, 2002; Limbos & Geva, 2001). Often teachers who overrefer ELs for special education evaluation label certain delays in academic performance or language as possible signs of a learning disability. Feeling ill equipped to evaluate whether or not these behaviors reflect the natural process of acquiring a second language, cultural issues, social/emotional issues, lack of opportunities to learn, and so on, teachers may quickly refer these students for evaluation for learning disabilities. Other teachers, more sensitive to second language issues, avoid referring ELs, especially during the early grades, for fear of labeling a child's linguistic status and learning differences as "disability." These students may, in fact, desperately need immediate and explicit assistance in learning to read or may require additional support in English language development. Many of these students eventually get referred for special education evaluation in the later grades. The result is they lose precious time to catch up with same-age peers and grade-level expectations. The reauthorization of the Individuals with Disabilities Education Improvement Act in 2004 attempted to remedy this "wait-and-fail" approach by allowing schools to emphasize early intervention on targeted skills using research-based methods and students' responsiveness to intervention as the means to determine eligibility for special education. What exactly do we know about how ELs respond to intense reading intervention?

The research on students' responsiveness to reading intervention is much more abundant for monolingual English speakers than for ELs. The National Literacy Panel's 2006 review of the research found only 17 studies that met their criteria for review of reading research involving ELs in comparison to the National Reading Panel's review in 2000 of more than 400 such studies involving native English speakers. Although scarce, reading intervention research on ELs has shown that these students do benefit from explicit small group reading intervention (Vaughn, Mathes, Linan-Thompson & Francis, 2005). ELs who struggle to acquire beginning reading skills and receive an appropriate core reading curriculum and research-based intervention yet fail to demonstrate gains may be candidates for special education evaluation. However, students who struggle with reading and classroom assessments yet are responsive to intense and explicit instruction in core reading skills may only need temporary support or remediation rather than special education services.

How can teachers more effectively support greater reading outcomes for young ELs? What are the necessary components of an effective early reading intervention for ELs? And how do these supports and practices differ from what is typically provided to monolingual English speakers? In order to answer these questions, we first provide a description of these students and the unique characteristics teachers should consider during intervention. Next, the content, instructional practices, and research related specifically to early reading development with ELs are presented.

Characteristics of English Learners

Individual Differences among English Learners

Teachers understand that students who come to school speaking a second language are a group of learners with potentially great differences. These students may vary in the amount of English they understand and can use in the classroom and the ease with which they develop literacy skills in a language they are only beginning to acquire. In order to work effectively with English learners (ELs), educators should understand general background characteristics, recognize the influence of a primary language in acquiring second language reading skills, and be able to differentiate a learning disability from typical second language development.

Many ELs may come to the United States for the first time during the early elementary school years (e.g., preschool, kindergarten) or further along in their education (e.g., middle school). Multiple variables can affect students' language and literacy outcomes, including the age at which children begin receiving second language instruction; parental education and socioeconomic status; home literacy practices and language models used in the home; the degree of similarity between first and second languages; and a child's intact cognitive, sensory, and motor skills for processing language and literacy skills (Kohnert, 2008). How can teachers recognize and address these students' unique needs within early reading intervention? To answer this question, we introduce three students—Marcos, Danilo, and Mina—all of whom have varying levels of English language proficiency and individual needs for reading support. Through these case examples, we demonstrate the variability among ELs and how to address their individual needs through reading intervention.

Marcos: Cultivating Phonological Awareness. Ms. Cowan, a reading specialist at Kentwood Elementary School, supports kindergarten, first-, and second-grade teachers. Most students at Kentwood in need of assistance include ELs. These students have varied instructional and linguistic backgrounds that directly impact their performance in reading. For example, Marcos, a kindergarten student in Ms. Rigs's classroom, recently came to Kentwood Elementary from Mexico City. He has strong Spanish language skills and virtually no expressive or receptive language skills in English. Through a careful interview with Marcos's parents and a home visit, both with an interpreter, Ms. Rigs discovered that Marcos attended preschool in Mexico and began to identify initial sounds in words, including his name and the names of important places within his community. Marcos's preschool program focused heavily on helping children sound out syllables in multisyllabic words and identify rhyming words informally through music and predictable stories. Ms. Rigs is well aware that these activities, although conducted in Spanish, will assist Marcos to acquire critical phonological awareness skills in English.

Research on ELs like Marcos has shown that general linguistic knowledge (Bialystok & Hakuta, 1994; Cummins, 1996) and literacy skills (Durgonoğlu, 2002) may exist as two components, one for common knowledge across languages and another for language-specific information. Common knowledge may allow skills in the stronger language to easily transfer to a second language; this is called **cross-linguistic transfer**. The question of most interest to practicing teachers like Ms. Rigs is whether or not existing skills accessible in a student's stronger, or native, language facilitate development of later word reading. "There is now growing research evidence of cross-language transfer in different literacy processes. . . . Some examples are phonological awareness, syntactic awareness, knowledge of genres and meaning-making strategies" (Durgonoğlu, 2002, pg. 189).

Specifically, phonological awareness skills developed in one language have been shown to transfer across languages and facilitate reading ability in the second language (Cisero & Royer, 1995; Durgonoğlu, Nagy & Hancin-Bhatt, 1993; Durgonoğlu, 1998; Leafstedt & Gerber, 2005). These results indicate that phonological awareness facilitates reading development regardless of the language of instruction (Bialystok, 2007). In other words, if students like Marcos develop phonological awareness in their stronger language, this process likely will facilitate development of the same skill in the second language (Durgonoğlu, 2002; Leafstedt & Gerber, 2005). Other common underlying proficiencies, such as working memory (the process for briefly storing and manipulating information), and well-developed oral and literacy skills in a first language can also assist English language literacy development in ELs (Genesee, Geva, Dressler & Kamil, 2006).

Ms. Cowan therefore encourages Ms. Rigs to continue working with Marcos on similar activities to further enhance his development of phonological awareness skills in English.

Danilo: Differentiating a Learning Disability. At Kentwood Elementary School, Ms. Cowan also provides support for Mrs. Harrison, a first-grade teacher experiencing difficulty with a boisterous six-year-old boy named Danilo, whose family is from the Philippines. Tagalog was Danilo's first language. He began acquiring English when he was four years old by listening to his brothers practice at home and by watching English television programs. Danilo, like many of his classmates, comes from a bilingual home with both adult and sibling models of English speaking. Many of Danilo's classmates come from similar linguistic and family backgrounds and attended kindergarten with Danilo the previous year. The program last year as well as the present year consists of English reading instruction; a rigorous English language develop-ment component; and primary language supports available through a bilingual paraprofessional, bilingual peers, and translated text when necessary.

From the first months of school through December, Mrs. Harrison has noticed that Danilo continues to struggle to learn the letters of the alphabet, identify words that rhyme and start with the same sound, and segment and blend three-phoneme words like *cat* and *sat*. Moreover, Danilo does not have as many expressive skills in English as do other students, and he needs directions repeated multiple times before he un-derstands what is being asked of him. Given his energetic personality, family language models, and number of bilingual and English-speaking friends in the classroom, it does not appear that Danilo's lack of lan-guage development in English can be attributed to few opportunities to hear appropriate English language models or participate in meaningful and safe conversations in English. Mrs. Harrison is not sure whether Danilo's difficulties in acquiring beginning reading skills are due to his acquisition of English, his second language, or a possible learning disability.

Mrs. Harrison consults with Ms. Cowan regarding next steps. Teachers and family members should compare a child experiencing language or learning difficulties with typically developing children with similar linguistic, educational, and familial backgrounds. Children with problems specifically in language may experience a delayed onset of language and possibly may be slow to learn the grammatical aspects of their primary language. These children will not learn verbal information at school or at home as quickly or as well as other students in the classroom (Genesee, Paradis & Crago, 2006).

Mrs. Harrison and Ms. Cowan feel that more information is necessary to determine whether Danilo's difficulties in reading and language are attributed to issues related to language development or an underlying disability. They carefully assess the factors presented in Table 3.1.

After consulting with Ms. Cowan, Mrs. Harrison plans to interview Danilo's parents regarding the development and use of his first language at home and to refer Danilo for a screening of his expressive and receptive language skills in both languages. Perhaps Danilo's difficulties stem from insufficient time acquiring English prior to formal reading instruction in English. Despite varying theoretical views regarding the minimum number of years necessary to develop proficiency in English in order for students to participate successfully in English reading (Baker, 1998; Krashen, 1996), there is consensus about the importance of developing oral English proficiency as part of the education of ELs (Genesee, Lindholm-Leary, Saunders & Christian, 2006). Focused and explicit intervention can assist in this process. Therefore, Mrs. Harrison plans to provide individualized or small group intervention instruction in phonological awareness, using words that include sounds found in both languages while explicitly emphasizing those sounds that are unique in English. Mrs. Harrison will monitor Danilo's progress on a weekly basis for the next 8 to 10 weeks to determine whether or not he is able to master oral English skills with additional support or whether more intense, specialized instruction is necessary.

TABLE 3.1 **Factors Differentiating Learning Disability from Difficulty in Second Language Acquisition**

Background to Consider

- Unusual delay in acquisition of primary language in comparison to the norm and to siblings or other family members

- History of learning disability within the family

- Academic difficulties experienced during primary language instruction, if provided

- Difficulties with primary language use and comprehension at home with the family

- Lack of progress when provided ongoing, intensive intervention in areas of need

Behaviors to Consider

- Unusual delay in acquiring second language

- Lack of progress in second language proficiency; limited vocabulary, with brief, short verbalizations in second language

- Difficulty retaining basic information from one day to the next

- Lack of comprehension of basic concepts, even with the assistance of bilingual materials, peers, or adults

Behaviors to Question

- Lack of expressive language in either language (possibly due to cultural, social/emotional factors)

- Weaknesses in academic skills as shown by a failure to respond to instruction in one or both languages (may be due to limited previous educational experiences, current inappropriate instruction, and/or cultural differences)

- Difficulties with articulation (possibly due to differences between first and second language)

Mina: Developing Vocabulary and Compehension.   Ms. Cowan also assists Mr. Watson, a second-grade classroom teacher at Kentwood Elementary School. Mr. Watson is having trouble supporting Mina, an eight-year-old student who is an English learner. Mina was born in the United States, but her parents emigrated from Iran and speak Farsi at home. Mina initially began speaking Farsi as her first language while acquiring English once she began kindergarten. Mr. Watson observes that Mina's informal conversational skills in English, both in the classroom and on the playground, are fairly strong. In the classroom, she frequently volunteers her thoughts and opinions without hesitating, using complete sentences, and is able to follow classroom routines smoothly. However, when she contributes orally in class, she occasionally needs more time to express her ideas correctly. At times, she uses terms or vocabulary inappropriately, and she often makes grammatical or word-order errors.

During intervention reading instruction, Mina tends to struggle with certain vocabulary and sight words and has trouble understanding what she reads. When required to read more **context-reduced material**, much like what is provided during science, math, and social studies instruction, she often has trouble putting her thoughts together. Her most recent oral reading fluency screening indicates that Mina is reading approximately 54 words correctly per minute in English on a benchmark reading passage done in December. She decodes most words correctly but struggles when having to read quickly. This places Mina at some risk for reading difficulty in the middle of the school year. Many students within this range of risk often have a 50 percent chance of either becoming increasingly at risk or of improving into the low-risk category. The result frequently depends on the level and quality of intervention provided, the adequacy of general core reading instruction, and the unique characteristics of the student.

With this information, Mr. Watson and Ms. Cowan conclude that Mina needs further support to develop her vocabulary and fluency skills and needs more attention on reading comprehension. During reading instruction, Mr. Watson decides to implement repeated reading and partner reading in order to improve her fluency. In addition to Mina's instruction in English language development, her teacher or a peer explicitly reviews high-frequency and sight words at the beginning of each lesson. Mina repeats these words out loud after hearing her teacher pronounce and briefly define them. Whenever possible, Mr.

Watson includes pictures corresponding with the words to reinforce word meanings.

As you can see, there is a lot of heterogeneity among ELs. These students may vary in their level of English and primary language skills, their familial and previous instructional experiences, and how they compare with same-age peers who are also ELs. Their unique linguistic, cultural, familial, academic, and instructional backgrounds can greatly influence their performance during intervention and continued development in English reading. Therefore, teachers who provide reading intervention during the early years of schooling must be knowledgeable about the appropriate content for reading intervention for ELs, and the additional intervention supports required to meet their unique needs.

Early Reading Instruction for English Learners

When considering what to teach English learners who are struggling with beginning literacy, the focus on the foundational skills of reading is essential. As described in Chapter 2, the National Reading Panel (2000) describes the five core components of reading as concepts and principles that facilitate the most efficient and broadest acquisition of knowledge across a range of examples in a domain. Native English speakers who do not master the core components of reading generally experience reading failure, so it follows that ELs may experience similar difficulties. Research results indicate that students who were provided with intensive and explicit intervention as a supplement to the core reading program outperformed comparison students on the foundation skills (Vaughn et al., 2006). Thus far what we have learned from the research is that these core skills apply to all readers, including ELs; however, certain adjustments in instruction must be made (Baker & Gersten, 1997; Gersten & Geva, 2003). The following guiding principles can assist teachers in purposefully shaping their instruction and strategies for EL reading intervention.

Guiding Principles for Intervention with English Learners

Support for English learners during reading in K-through-2 classrooms provides focused, intensive, small group intervention in the core reading areas of phonological awareness, phonics, and reading fluency. Interventions need to be explicit, use direct instruction techniques, and be delivered in small groups. Strong recommendations come out of the report on *Effective Literacy and English Language Instruction for ELs in the Elementary Grades* (Gersten et al., 2007) to support explicit reading instruction. These include

1. Use an intervention program that includes instructional principles that give students multiple opportunities to respond to questions and practice reading both words and sentences while teachers give students immediate and clear feedback when they make errors.

2. Dedicate at least 30 minutes daily for small group intervention.

3. Provide ongoing training and support for all personnel providing intervention.

4. Provide vocabulary instruction by teaching content words in addition to teaching more common words, phrases, and expressions necessary for school success that students have yet to learn.

Given these principles of good classroom teaching procedures and instruction, what does effective reading intervention with ELs look like? Reading intervention for ELs, as for monolingual English-speaking peers, can effectively be provided within a three-tier model of primary, secondary, and tertiary instruction (Haager, Calhoon & Linan-Thompson, 2007). Primary intervention, or tier1, is the core reading program that every student receives in school. Secondary intervention, or tier 2, refers to the added daily 30 minutes of focused and explicit instruction that some students may need. Tertiary intervention, tier 3, refers to an additional daily 30-minute intervention period that is delivered one on one and that is over and above the primary and secondary intervention periods for general education students. Once a structure for reading intervention is in place, what are the unique strategies for early reading intervention for ELs?

Strategies for Early Reading Intervention with English Learners

When effective intervention strategies are in place in the classroom, the core reading program is then accessible to English learners. Following are some suggestions for planning lessons in reading intervention for ELs that include the core components of reading.

Phonological Awareness Interventions. PA is a skill with cross-linguistic transfer; that is, a student who has PA in one language will be able to apply that skill to his or her second language. Students will be able to easily demonstrate this skill initially in English using those sounds that are similar to their first language. An example of this would be using a word whose initial sound is the same in the primary language as in English (e.g., /l/ as in *light* makes the same sound in Spanish). When teaching PA to an English learner, use the same strategies and techniques that you use with monolingual students. Additional modeling and limiting of teacher talk will assist the student in understanding the task and will allow for additional practice. Students unfamiliar with the sound system of a new language need to be able to hear appropriate modeling of sounds in words. Remember: the ultimate goal in PA is for the student to hear the individual sounds in words and to repeat them orally.

Studies with ELs on these and similar strategies show resultant reading gains. Defior and Tudela (1994), for example, studied first-graders during intervention to measure their mastery of phoneme discrimination (e.g., /p/, /d/) versus picture-sound association (e.g., *boat*, *ball* = /b/). Some of the intervention tasks were conducted using manipulatives. Results indicated that when using plastic letters coupled with letter sounds, first-graders improved in both reading and writing skills. These results further support the practice of teaching the phonological sounds and letter symbols simultaneously when working with ELs. In another study, instructors used picture cards representing words beginning with the same sound for the purpose of teaching word onsets and rimes with EL kindergarteners. Students orally blended onset and rime components (e.g., *b-at*, *c-at*, *m-an*, etc.) and segmented words into individual sounds while manipulating hands-on letter tiles (Leafstedt, Richards & Gerber, 2004). By the end of the year, participating students met monolingual English benchmarks for word reading. Overall, these and other findings support coupling PA interventions with visual and kinesthetic aids for EL students

Alphabetic Principle Interventions. The alphabetic principle, or phonics, should be taught to ELs using linguistic patterns and bringing meaning to words when at all possible. Getting bogged down in rules can detract from the student's understanding of how these words fit into context. Interventions using the alphabetic principle should include teaching letter knowledge to develop automatic recognition of a letter symbol and the most common sound it represents. An effective method for teaching this skill with ELs is to use cognates, or words that have a common spelling and meaning across languages. For example, the English-Spanish cognates *police—policia, bank—banco,* and *map—mapa* might be used to teach the letter sounds /p/, /b/, and /m/. Furthermore, when teaching beginning word recognition in English, ELs can learn to sound out phonetically regular high-frequency words through the use of linguistic patterns and then to move from syllables to whole words (Vaughn et al., 2006). Examples of patterned single-syllable words include the following:

be	he	me	she	we
an	can	ran		
got	hot	not		
ate	make	take		
see	green	keep	sleep	three

Each word set contains a core phonics pattern that students can use to generalize to other words, even multisyllabic words, using similar sound patterns. Additionally, learners need to recognize with some degree of automaticity phonetically irregular high-frequency words such as *two, buy,* and *laugh*. During intervention, using word walls, and flashcards with corresponding pictures, while giving multiple opportunities for repeated reading, can be useful in teaching students irregular high-frequency words.

Fluency Interventions. Much as for monolingual English speakers, lesson activities to enhance ELs' fluency skills require that students use familiar text so difficult sounds and words are practiced and comprehension is achieved. Repeated reading is one of the most salient interventions to develop fluency with connected text (Denton, 2000; Malloy, Gilbertson & Maxfield, 2007; NRP, 2000). Students practice daily reading of decodable text in order to improve rate and accuracy. Accurate decoding and reading lead to improved comprehension; when more time is spent on phonics interventions, reading fluency improves (Haager, Dimino & Windmueller, 2007).

In addition to the examples previously described, research on early reading for ELs strongly concludes that the explicit and redundant nature of intervention instruction provides the support students need to make adequate progress (Gersten & Geva, 2003; Linan-Thompson, Vaughn, Prater & Cirino, 2006). Repetitive procedures for problem solving and task completion should be explicitly taught and scaffolded from simple to more complex tasks. Established procedures assist ELs to focus on intervention content. It should be noted that instruction in the foundational skills of phonological awareness and phonics is more crucial in the beginning stages of reading and less important as students become more proficient readers of connected texts. As students begin to make meaning of what they are reading, they rely less on sounding out words (Gerber et al., 2004; Leafstedt, Richards & Gerber, 2004).

Vocabulary Interventions. Finally, although we have not addressed vocabulary intervention explicitly, it is important to note that language support modifications—such as the use of visuals, gestures, and facial expressions—are important when teaching ELs vocabulary and oracy skills (Vaughn et al., 2006). Additional methods of supporting vocabulary during intervention include previewing target words, reinforcing word meanings with pictures, requiring students to repeat words modeled by the teacher, and using words in sentences. Overall, reading intervention for ELs must do more than develop a complex array of reading skills as outlined previously. There must also be a synchronized effort to increase the scope and complexity of students' oral language proficiency to ensure greater gains (Shanahan & Beck, 2006). Interventions that support oral language improvement assist students to outperform peer groups not receiving oral language support during intervention (Linan-Thompson, Cirino & Vaughn, 2007).

Supplemental Instruction to Support Intervention with English Learners

This chapter focuses exclusively on early reading intervention for English learners. At minimum, teachers must recognize both the principles and content of intervention instruction critical for supporting beginning reading development with ELs. Beyond this essential foundation, other methods of instruction and support must be provided for ELs to make

---

TABLE 3.2   ELD Classroom Strategies that Support Intervention

Teaching Strategies	Classroom Environment
Preteaching vocabulary, either the day before or prior to the daily lesson	**Providing a print-rich classroom environment** that gives students the needed scaffolds to refer to for immediate assistance throughout the school day
Tape recording the story of the day so that EL students can listen repeatedly	**Setting up the classroom** so that there is space for you to work with a small group of students during the day when conducting intervention
Using choral or echo reading to help students become familiar with new text	**Providing students with enough "wait time"** to process their answers and develop an appropriate response to questions
Making sure that students are using accountable talk, both with teachers and peers; accountable talk encourages students to have conversations about text in which they can respond to peers and adults and truly articulate their thinking	**Including word walls, posted vocabulary lists, sound-spelling cards, and word boxes** containing previously taught vocabulary and flashcards on a ring for quick reference

TABLE 3.3 Home-School Connections That Support Reading Intervention

Practices	Description	Examples
Family outreach	Teachers facilitate active parent participation and tap into parents' knowledge and experiences.	• Survey parents at the beginning of the year regarding their availability for volunteering in the classroom and their knowledge/implementation of effective home literacy practices. • Invite parents into the classroom to manage independent learning groups during intervention instruction. • Invite parents to work individually with students reading passages, practicing with sight words, building words, and so on.
School-based reading activities in the home	Teachers encourage parents to implement activities in the home that mimic and reinforce teachers' instruction of early reading skills.	• Play rhyming games. • Use magnetic letters and words to create simple words and sentences. • Use letter or word tiles to create words and sentences. • Read and discuss storybooks.
Everyday reading activities in the home	Teachers encourage parents to engage in practices that are more meaningful and authentic.	• Engage in oral conversations and stories. • Write and dictate letters/cards to friends and relatives. • Read signs on the street and labels in stores. • Translate signs, notes, and messages.

sufficient gains in core reading skills. Not only do ELs need explicit teaching in the core components of reading, but they also need specific strategies for English language development (ELD). There should be a strong general focus on oral language proficiency and learning vocabulary at a deeper level of processing, and students should be provided multiple opportunities to practice newly acquired skills (Windmueller, 2004). Some ELD classroom strategies that frame and support intervention work with EL students are included in Table 3.2.

In addition to effective ELD instruction, educators can maximize the benefits of a good core reading program and intervention instruction for ELs by fostering greater home-school connections. "Existing research suggests that parent/family factors have an impact on the literacy development of language minority students, and parents are often willing to help their children succeed academically" (Goldenberg, Rueda & August, 2006, p. 263). Even when conducted in a student's primary language, home literacy activities can facilitate transfer of important skills into a second language (in this case, English). Table 3.3 provides some examples of how teachers can encourage parent participation and home literacy practices in order to produce greater reading gains with ELs

Summary

English learners vary greatly along several factors, including language proficiency, previous and current educational experiences, and cultural and socioeconomic background. Like all children, ELs differ in areas related to cognition, learning, memory, intelligence, and motivation (TESOL, 2007). These differences can make it difficult for ELs to acquire necessary reading skills in a second language. Some ELs who experience early reading failure have trouble accessing needed services, which can cause them to fall farther behind. For other ELs, special education referral, evaluation, and placement have become all too commonplace. Fortunately, changes in special and general education legislation allow educators to provide early intervention in reading for struggling learners in general education programs rather than permit continued academic failure.

Reading intervention research with ELs, although scarce, emphasizes the importance of providing explicit instruction in skill areas critical for developing word reading-skills. Although this literature often supports the application of many of the same instructional strategies and methods valid for monolingual students, the methods, when appropriately modified for ELs, can produce positive outcomes in reading.

The authors would like to thank Skye Fraser for all her research and work on this chapter.

Reading Intervention for Students with Learning Disabilities

Terese C. Aceves and Diane Haager

Objectives

By the end of this chapter, the reader will be able to

1. Describe characteristics of students who are likely
have a learning disability (LD) and those who
are just struggling readers, as well as how these
student characteristics differ

2. Discuss the essential components of reading
intervention for students with LD, both content
and methods of intervention

3. List and describe the common models for providing
reading intervention for students with LD

The federal definition of learning disabilities has remained virtually
unchanged since it first became part of federal policy in 1975
with the passage of the Education for All Handicapped Children
Act, or P.L. 94-142. The condition of learning disabilities has been defined as a disorder in psychological processes that "may manifest itself
in an imperfect ability to listen, think, read, write, spell or to do mathe-
matical calculations." Until recently, this definition was widely inter-
preted as the "discrepancy model," requiring the Individual Education
Program, or IEP team, to verify that a significant discrepancy exists
between a student's intellectual and academic functioning. Under this
model, the referral and identification process of students for special education services has become extremely problematic. Specifically, subjec-
tivity in the referral process, flawed or inadequate tests, and ambiguous
criteria are often cited as contributing factors in the misidentification of
students as having learning disabilities (Vaughn & Klingner, 2007).
Moreover, students with learning disabilities have typically had to wait
until third or fourth grade, sometimes beyond, for testing to show a
wide enough gap in performance to qualify for special education. Under
these conditions, students often fall hopelessly behind their peers and
rarely catch up, despite special education services.

Response to intervention (RTI; see Chapter 1) may help teachers
discriminate between a struggling learner and a student with a significant learning disability in the early grades. The current law (IDEIA,

2004, P.L. 108-466) allows schools to use a process of examining the child's responsiveness to "scientific, research-based intervention" for determining if a child has a specific learning disability and is eligible to receive special education. The federal regulations indicate that the school must provide documentation of the instructional strategies used and student data that show a lack of responsiveness to instruction.

This chapter begins by reviewing the unique characteristics of students with learning disabilities using student examples to distinguish a struggling learner from a learner with an identified disability in reading. We review interventions for elementary school students with reading disabilities, including research supporting the content and methods of instruction. Finally, the chapter concludes with an outline specifying existing models of service delivery that teachers may encounter in the schools and the roles and responsibilities of both general and special educators within these structures.

49

Chapter Four
Reading
Intervention for
Students with
Learning
Disabilities

Identifying Students with Learning Disabilities

Ms. Garcia, a first-grade teacher, is concerned about Marty. Despite daily supplemental reading instruction, he continues to lag behind in basic reading skills. In checking his history, Ms. Garcia finds that Marty's kindergarten teacher was also concerned. She thinks he may have a learning disability but is not sure whether his difficulties are serious enough to warrant taking his case to the Student Study Team. The legal guidelines for identifying students with learning disabilities (LD) have been confusing to many over the years. Students with learning disabilities make up a heterogeneous group of children whose disorders may manifest differently. How can teachers distinguish between struggling readers and students with LD? What signs would Ms. Garcia look for in determining whether to make a referral for Marty?

Students like Marty, who experience difficulties in academic functioning such as reading, have often been considered for special education placement, but the procedures used for determining a discrepancy between intellectual and academic functioning have been controversial. According to the discrepancy model, Marty's reading performance would have to be significantly below some measure of cognitive functioning for him to qualify for special education. Ms. Garcia alone cannot determine this; she will need the help of a multidisciplinary team that includes a school psychologist qualified to give cognitive tests. Another complication in Marty's case is the "wait-and-fail" phenomenon (Vaughn & Klingner, 2007) in which the discrepancy between academic and cognitive functioning is not typically apparent in the early years of schooling. In the early stages of academic development, all students would score at low levels academically, because they are at the starting point of developing basic academic skills. Existing tests are not sensitive enough to pick up a significant lag in performance until typical grade-level performance is more advanced, at least at the second-grade level or beyond. In order to have a significant discrepancy, students usually need to score more than a year below grade level. Therefore, by the time academic tests can pick up a lag in performance that is significant, a student who truly has a learning disability has experienced the wait-and-fail phenomenon, experiencing difficulty for two or more years until tests can document a severe learning difficulty.

According to a response-to-intervention approach, Ms. Garcia must provide systematic, supplemental instruction that can be documented in case it is needed for eligibility procedures. She must also collect on-going student data (e.g., oral reading fluency probes) to support her assumption that Marty is lagging behind despite appropriate intervention. Marty would only be considered to have a learning disability if he does not respond to "scientifically-based intervention" provided as supplemental to the core academic program. To distinguish whether Marty is a struggling reader or has a learning disability, Ms. Garcia must provide research-based reading intervention and note Marty's response to the intervention. A struggling reader will likely respond positively to the intervention (tier 2) and get back on track; a student with a learning disability will likely need more intensive support provided by a special education teacher (tier 3).

What steps should Ms. Garcia take to further explore Marty's reading difficulties and determine if he does or does not have a learning disability? There are two primary components of the RTI approach that involve general education teachers: assessment and intervention. These procedures are most effective in a preventive, proactive RTI model when they are used systematically and schoolwide. Teachers at every grade would use screening assessments to identify struggling learners as candidates for supplemental intervention. After providing systematic intervention, progress-monitoring assessments would provide documentation of the student's responsiveness to the instruction.

Struggling Readers in the Primary Grades

51

Chapter Four
Reading
Intervention for
Students with
Learning
Disabilities

Teachers in the primary grades have an important role in ensuring the success of students who experience difficulty with learning, regardless of whether the cause is a learning disability or simply difficulty with learning. What indicators would a teacher look for to identify students who need intervention and support?

Because of the RTI provision in the IDEIA law, schools are increasingly adopting systematic assessment systems to aid in identifying and monitoring struggling students. Universal screening procedures are being implemented in which all students are assessed on a regular basis (at the beginning of the school year, followed by periodic checks) to determine which students may need supplemental intervention. Children who perform below grade-level benchmarks (relative to a norming sample) are candidates for intervention. Speece and Walker (2007) warn of finding "false positives," or identifying students for intervention who may actually be performing adequately. Using teacher observation and judgment in tandem with screening may reduce overidentification of students for intervention, and careful progress monitoring following identification will identify any students who are truly making adequate grade-level progress.

Following are descriptions of two students identified in first grade, through screening assessments, as needing supplemental intervention. We will see how their schools examined the students' response to intervention to determine if these students needed further evaluation for learning disability.

Marissa's school uses the Dynamic Indicators of Basic Early Literacy Skills (DIBELS) assessment system to systematically screen and monitor student progress in kindergarten through fifth grades (Good & Kaminski, 2002). At the beginning of the school year, Marissa scored in the intensive range, or highly at risk, in three key skill areas. Marissa's scores are listed in Table 4.1. By the middle of first grade, following six weeks of supplemental intervention, Marissa had moved into the strategic range in phonological awareness (segmenting phonemes) and alphabetic principle (phonetic decoding), skills that are heavily emphasized in the first-grade curriculum and were targeted in the supplemental intervention. Though Marissa is still in the intensive range in reading fluency at midyear, there is evidence that she is responding to the intervention. She has shown significant growth in phonological awareness and decoding. Her teacher, Ms. Flowers, has assessed her

TABLE 4.1 Marissa's DIBELS Scores, Grade 1

DIBELS Subtest	DIBELS Scoring Rubric for Determining Instruction	Fall Score and Recommendation	Winter Score and Recommendation	Spring Score and Recommendation
Letter Naming Fluency (rapid letter identification)	< 25 Intensive 25–36 Strategic 37 Benchmark met	15 Intensive	Not given[a]	Not given
Phoneme Segmentation Fluency (phonemic awareness)	< 10 Intensive 10–34 Strategic 35 Benchmark met	0 Intensive	13 Strategic	38 Benchmark met
Nonsense Word Fluency (alphabetic principle)	*Beginning Grade 1* < 13 Intensive 13–23 Strategic 24 Benchmark met *Middle and End of Grade 1* < 30 Intensive 30–49 Strategic 50 Benchmark met	4 Intensive	34 Strategic	53 Benchmark met
Oral Reading Fluency (fluent passage reading)	*Middle Grade 1* < 8 Intensive 8–19 Strategic 20 Benchmark met *End Grade 1* < 20 Intensive 20–39 Strategic 40 Benchmark met		5 Intensive	27 Strategic

[a]The DIBELS system does not use the Letter Naming test beyond the beginning of the year.

weekly using the DIBELS Oral Reading Fluency assessment. It was evident a few weeks into the intervention phase that Marissa was responding positively to the intervention. Figure 4.1 shows her graphed progress-monitoring assessment in the area of phonetic decoding. Marissa's progress approximates the line from her starting point to the goal. This indicates steady progress and the likelihood of reaching the benchmark by the end of the year. A positive response to intervention by the midyear screening assessment means that Marissa likely does not have a learning disability but instead is a student who needs extra support in acquiring basic reading skills. At midyear, her teacher may change the focus of the intervention to build Marissa's fluency but will also continue to reinforce decoding and phonological awareness. Additional information from informal assessments and teacher observation can enhance Ms. Flower's ability to adjust the intervention to meet Marissa's specific needs within a small group setting.

53

Chapter Four

Reading
Intervention for
Students with
Learning
Disabilities

FIGURE 4.1   Marissa's Progress-Monitoring Chart for Nonsense Word Fluency

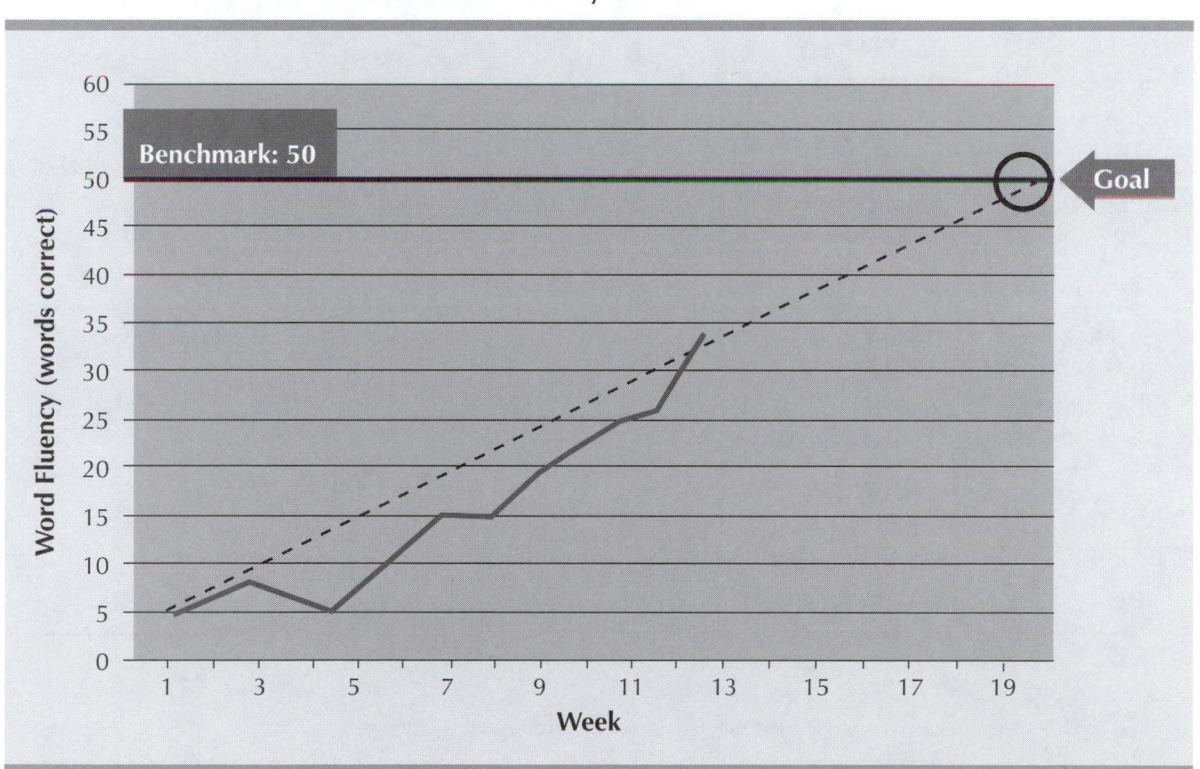

TABLE 4.2 Jonathan's DIBELS Scores, Grade 1

DIBELS Subtest	DIBELS Scoring Rubric for Determining Instruction	Fall Score and Recommendation	Winter Score and Recommendation	Spring Score and Recommendation
Letter Naming Fluency (rapid letter identification)	< 25 Intensive 25–36 Strategic 37 Benchmark met	18 Intensive	Not given[a]	Not given
Phoneme Segmentation Fluency (phonemic awareness)	< 10 Intensive 10–34 Strategic 35 Benchmark met	4 Intensive	8 Intensive	10 Strategic
Nonsense Word Fluency (alphabetic principle)	*Beginning Grade 1* < 13 Intensive 13–23 Strategic 24 Benchmark met *Middle and End Grade 1* < 30 Intensive 30–49 Strategic 50 Benchmark met	7 Intensive	9 Intensive	23 Intensive
Oral Reading Fluency (fluent passage reading)	*Middle Grade 1* < 8 Intensive 8–19 Strategic 20 Benchmark met *End Grade 1* < 20 Intensive 20–39 Strategic 40 Benchmark met		0 Intensive	8 Intensive

[a]The DIBELS system does not use the Letter Naming test beyond the beginning of the year.

Jonathan, another first-grader showing early signs of difficulty, has a beginning-of-year profile similar to Marissa's. However, he does not show the same rate of progress as Marissa. Is he a likely candidate for a referral for consideration for special education?

Table 4.2 summarizes Jonathan's scores over the year. At the beginning-of-year screening, his scores put him in the intensive range in three areas: rapid letter naming, segmenting phonemes, and phonetic decoding. Unlike Marissa, however, the midyear testing does not show any significant growth, despite Jonathan's participation in an intervention program. In fact, Jonathan continues to struggle in the intensive range in the key skills of phonological awareness and the alphabetic principle. Figure 4.2 shows Jonathan's progress-monitoring graph up to midyear. Jonathan's progress falls well below the line from his starting point to the goal. This indicates a lack of progress and the

55

Chapter Four
Reading
Intervention for
Students with
Learning
Disabilities

FIGURE 4.2   Jonathan's Progress-Monitoring Chart for Nonsense Word Fluency

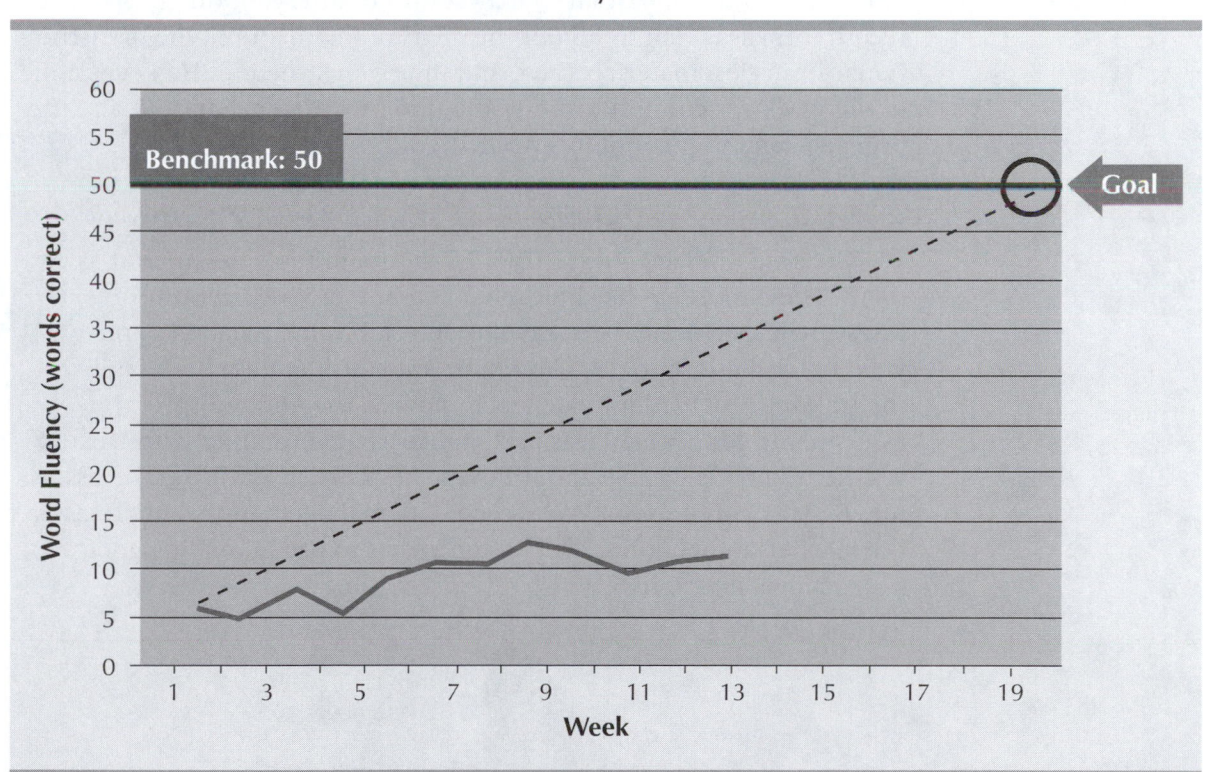

likelihood of his falling short of the benchmark by the end of the year. At this point, it is important for Jonathan's teacher, Mr. Oakley, and the school's Student Study Team to consider several important questions.

1. *Has Jonathan received consistent intervention that is supplemental to the core instructional program? Is there evidence that consistent, research-based intervention was provided?*

Mr. Oakley has scheduled small group intervention for struggling readers and has consistently provided intervention. This instruction is supplemental to the core instructional program in reading and occurs right after the core program time block. During this time, he organizes independent work and study centers so that most students are occupied with independent practice or writing. Early in the year, Mr. Oakley placed Jonathan in a group of four students who needed supplemental intervention based on their initial screening data. Because the IDEIA regulations stipulate that schools must present evidence at an IEP meeting of the implementation of research-based intervention for any student considered for special education placement, the school requires that Mr. Oakley maintain a weekly record of intervention groups. The record form asks him to fill out the areas of instruction, type of instructional strategies, materials used, and time of instruction. He keeps a file of the weekly records and shows them to the Student Study Team, the principal, and the parents, as needed.

2. *Was Jonathan's progress measured by valid and reliable assessment tools?*

The school selected the DIBELS assessment tools for student assessment. These tools are used for screening and progress-monitoring assessment specifically because of their established reliability and validity for these purposes. An important consideration in reliability is the training provided for teachers in how to use and interpret the assessments. Mr. Oakley was part of districtwide training with DIBELS, and he is knowledgeable about how to administer and score the assessments. The school uses a Web-based data management system to assist the teachers in obtaining reports and charts to use in making good instructional decisions.

3. Is the referral decision based on multiple measures and teacher observation?

In addition to the DIBELS assessments, Mr. Oakley has collected the assessments he conducted that his school district requires, such as the Developmental Reading Assessment (DRA). Jonathan showed consistent difficulty grasping key concepts in reading. Samples of Jonathan's writing and spelling assignments provide supporting evidence of his struggles with basic reading skills.

4. Were Jonathan's parents consulted regarding his intervention status?

Mr. Oakley met with Jonathan's parents early in the year following the screening assessment and initial round of assessment in the core reading program. He communicated with Jonathan's parents several times either by phone or e-mail to report progress, and he sent home Jonathan's monthly progress-monitoring chart. Mr. Oakley has kept consistent records of each communication.

Because Mr. Oakley has fulfilled each of the above requirements, there is ample evidence that Jonathan is not responding to the intervention as desired. He is in danger of failing to meet grade-level benchmarks by the end of the year. However, this may not yet be sufficient justification for making a referral to consider special education. This decision must be made on a case-by-case basis, in consultation with the parents, the school's Student Study Team, and the administrator. Mr. Oakley and the school team must be sure that Jonathan has had an opportunity to make progress. The school team may suggest a change in intervention to see if it might change Jonathan's trend of nonresponse. There is no set time frame for deciding that a student's lack of progress constitutes a nonresponse. Jonathan's current profile suggests that he is a likely candidate for a referral due to a nonresponse pattern, but the decision has not yet been made to make a formal referral. Meanwhile, Jonathan is receiving intensive intervention support so that he may not fall too far behind during his first-grade year.

Struggling Readers in the Upper Elementary Grades

Having a response-to-intervention approach to prevention and early identification is very helpful for students who struggle with reading acquisition, whether or not they have learning disabilities. Students

57

Chapter Four
Reading
Intervention for
Students with
Learning
Disabilities

with no significant learning disabilities but who experience some difficulty with early reading benefit from the early identification and intervention provided by RTI, as in the case of Marissa above. Students with true, innate learning disabilities also benefit from having a prevention model in place, because early intervention services may keep them from falling significantly behind.

For example, Roberto is a fifth-grader with a specific learning disability that impacts his academic learning. He has attended Eastside Elementary School since kindergarten. He repeated kindergarten due to difficulties with attention and acquiring basic prereading and math skills. In first grade, Eastside Elementary adopted a schoolwide plan for RTI. Despite supplemental small group reading instruction provided by his teacher throughout first grade, Roberto finished the year significantly behind in reading and mathematics. Early in the second grade, Roberto's teacher and the Student Study Team began the referral process that led to his designation as having learning disabilities and placement into special education services.

Roberto began the second grade with special education services in place in an inclusive service delivery model. He had already had quite a bit of extra assistance through the RTI process. During first grade, he had consistent supplemental reading intervention almost daily. In addition, his first-grade teacher provided extra support in a small group setting in math to help him learn the basic math facts and concepts. From second grade on, Roberto had access to the core instructional program through planned accommodations worked out collaboratively by his general and special education teachers. In the general education setting, Roberto continued to participate in the supplemental reading intervention and progress monitoring. Additionally, his special education teacher provided intensive specialized reading instruction using an alternative curriculum that focused on explicit, systematic instruction.

In the fifth grade, Roberto's instructional reading level is in the upper-third-grade to lower-fourth-grade range. His oral reading fluency scores using fourth-grade passages range from 80 to 95 words per minute, slow for a fifth-grader but fast enough so that he can comprehend what he reads. He struggles with multisyllabic decoding and complex concepts. His math performance continues to lag behind his peers. Still, this profile is different from what it might have been without the RTI supports in place. Prior to RTI, students such as Roberto would be subject to the wait-and-fail model of identification. In other words, without RTI, Roberto would have experienced prolonged failure until his discrepancy was severe enough to be documented by standardized tests; he probably would not have been identified until fourth grade. With RTI in place, Roberto is only a year or so behind in reading and is able to function within the general education curriculum with some accommodations for his slow pace and multisyllabic decoding difficulties. Without the support and intervention provided throughout his elementary grades, Roberto would likely have low motivation and other social/emotional issues resulting from experiencing an extended period of severe failure.

59

Chapter Four
Reading
Intervention for
Students with
Learning
Disabilities

Reading Intervention for Elementary Students with Learning Disabilities

Recognizing the difference between struggling readers and students with genuine learning disabilities in the area of reading is critical during the early years of schooling. Teachers must be able to **differentiate** between these students in order to provide the most appropriate services and supports as soon as possible. For example, Marissa, although identified as being at risk at the beginning of her first-grade year, made sufficient gains after receiving small group intervention instruction over a six-week period. Given her positive response to intervention, Marissa's teacher may discontinue further intervention and continue to monitor her progress within the core reading curriculum. However, Jonathan, who struggled similarly at the beginning of first grade, was unresponsive to supplemental reading instruction and demonstrated similar difficulties on school-based assessments of core reading concepts. His teacher most likely will present this documentation to the Student Study Team and refer Jonathan for further evaluation for a possible learning disability. Students who qualify for special education services given a mild-to-moderate learning disability affecting the area of reading most often will continue to receive their primary instruction within the general education classroom. Special education legislation mandates now more than ever that students with disabilities be educated within the least restrictive environment (IDEA, 1997; IDEIA, 2004) alongside nondisabled peers. In order to adequately address the needs of students serviced within general education programs, teachers should design unique reading programs to support learners with and without disabilities (Jiménez, Graf & Rose, 2007). How might the content of reading instruction differ for students with and without disabilities? Which methods of reading instruction have proven most effective in helping students with disabilities catch up to their nondisabled peers?

Content of Reading Instruction

Teachers should understand that the content of instruction for learners with LD reflects those essential reading skills identified by the National Reading Panel (2000). This includes instruction in phonological awareness, phonics, fluency, comprehension, and vocabulary across a range of grade and age levels. (Refer to Chapter 2.) Most teachers recognize that students identified with LD in the earlier grades should have explicit and regular instruction in these skill areas, depending on their individual needs. Unfortunately, educators often mistakenly assume that focusing on beginning reading skills no longer applies with older students with LD. The concern often centers exclusively on older students' difficulty with comprehension of text. "Not only do [older learners with LD] differ significantly from one another in their levels of reading difficulty, but they also differ in the nature of their reading problems" (Torgesen et al., 2001, p. 67). Many older learners with LD may still lack effective decoding strategies, which inevitably impacts text comprehension. Other older students may have adequate decoding skills, but deficiencies in vocabulary knowledge and reading fluency or speed may cause them to struggle to comprehend the passages they read. Teachers may describe their reading as accurate yet laborious and slow. All efforts are focused exclusively on decoding words on the page. Other older learners with LD may have accurate and fluent decoding ability yet lack essential strategies used by more efficient readers for comprehending text. Therefore, given the range of problems students with LD may experience, the content of instruction for younger and older students with LD will vary, depending on individual needs and strengths, and reflect the NRP's (2000) recommendations of what is essential for developing successful readers.

Methods of Instruction

As they mature (grade 2 and beyond), more time is necessary for students with LD to make gains in comparison to nondisabled at risk peers (Fletcher, Lyons, Fuchs & Barnes, 2007). Specifically, struggling learners and those with LD must make more than a year's growth on average in reading in comparison to their nondisabled same-age peers. Therefore, methods of instruction must be designed to assist with this type of growth (Torgesen et al., 2001). According to their review of the research in this area, Fletcher and colleagues (2007) drew 10 conclusions about the methods of intervention for students with LD and how to specifically enhance academic outcomes. These include

61

Chapter Four
Reading
Intervention for
Students with
Learning
Disabilities

1. Increasing students' time on task

2. Providing explicit, well-organized instruction with opportunities for cumulative review of previously mastered content

3. Specifically teaching academic skills and content

4. Teaching self-regulation strategies that hold students accountable for monitoring their own academic progress

5. Monitoring student progress frequently and relating such monitoring to intervention directly

6. Providing opportunities for engagement and practice within an "integrated" program

7. Providing opportunities for peer-assisted learning

8. Integrating foundational and higher-order skills systematically throughout instruction

9. Considering the heterogeneity of students with LD when designing and implementing remediation instruction

10. Systematically integrating interventions with general education practices

General and special educators should consider these important principles when designing, implementing, and evaluating their reading instruction of students with LD. Although all are important, we specifically highlight methods of intervention related to a few of these principles. These methods include use of direct instruction and corrective feedback, progress monitoring, and strategy instruction.

Direct Instruction. Direct instruction refers to the implementation of explicit, systematic, fast-paced teaching practices found to be effective with students experiencing difficulty in reading and those with reading-related disabilities. Within this approach students actively participate in interactive small group lessons, an essential component of instruction with struggling learners (NRP, 2000; Vaughn, Gersten & Chard, 2000). This approach emphasizes the assessment, instruction, and modification of observable behaviors. Direct instruction comprises seven critical features: an explicit step-by-step strategy, development of mastery at each step in the process, a process for correction of student errors, gradual fading from teacher-directed activities toward independent work, use of adequate and systematic practice with a range of examples, increased opportunities for student responses, and cumulative review of newly learned concepts (Gersten, Carnine & Woodward, 1987). (Chapter 6 discusses how these methods apply specifically to early reading skills.)

These features form the basis of the original instructional program (Direct Instruction, or DI) developed by Englemann and colleagues at the University of Oregon (Adams & Carnine, 2003). Other curricular programs with a more precise adoption of these features, including Reading Mastery (Engelmann & Bruner, 1997) and Corrective Reading (Engelmann, Hanner & Haddox, 1980), incorporate precisely scripted materials. Research on the use of Direct Instruction methods involving students with and without disabilities supports the effectiveness of this approach (Adams & Engelmann, 1996; White, 1988). In a comprehensive review of 300 studies using DI methods while including students with LD, Adams and Carnine (2003) found large effects in students' reading outcomes.

An instructional technique incorporated within typical DI sessions, yet difficult to implement consistently and effectively, is the use of ongoing teacher corrective feedback during instruction (Chard, Vaughn & Tyler, 2002; Gerber et al., 2004; Gersten & Geva, 2003; Kouri, Selle & Riley, 2006; Nelson, Alber & Gordy, 2004; Vaughn et al., 2005, 2006). Most teachers are accustomed to providing general verbal feedback during whole and small group instruction with all students; however, specific, corrective feedback becomes absolutely essential for students with LD to learn new skills, maintain and generalize their learning, and make sufficient gains overall.

Teacher feedback can be as diverse as students' responses during instruction. The type of corrective feedback a teacher provides depends heavily on students' intervention reading goals. Feedback should provide students with immediate responses, be brief and explicit, and require active and correct responses from students. Ongoing or sustained feedback can guide a struggling reader through the completion of a difficult task using "feed forward" behaviors (e.g., suggestions, praise, prompts and questions, and visual and verbal cues) (Cole, 2006). Sustained teacher feedback may involve requiring a student to expand on or explain a response (e.g., "How did you get that answer?"). Teachers may offer ongoing praise when appropriate and explain the reason for that praise (e.g., "Great job! I liked the way you read the parts of the word you already knew how to read.").

Research involving students with LD includes corrective feedback as an essential component of intervention instruction. Specifically, in their review of 24 studies examining error corrections and oral reading, Heubusch and Lloyd (1998) determined that corrective feedback improved students' reading accuracy. Studies involving English learners (Gerber et al., 2004; Vaughn et al., 2005, 2006) and students with learning disabilities (Nelson, Alber & Gordy, 2004) have continued to demonstrate positive effects on students' reading skills. (See Chapter 6 for more information on corrective feedback.)

Progress Monitoring. Generally effective reading interventions are not necessarily effective for all students. Formative evaluation, which uses ongoing assessment to inform instruction and is widely implemented in reading intervention, is necessary to assist teachers in being responsive to students' needs by modifying and improving intervention strategies for individual students (Deno, 1986). Ongoing assessment, or progress monitoring, through curriculum-based measurement (CBM; Deno, 2003) provides teachers with the immediate feedback necessary regarding individual students' progress during intervention. (See Chapter 7 for more information on progress monitoring and CBM.)

Monitoring progress is an essential component of any instructional program for students with disabilities. The process of monitoring student progress toward goal attainment includes four essential steps: collecting initial assessment data or information prior to initiating a new intervention or strategy, setting instructional and learning goals, initiating instruction, and collecting progress monitoring data of student performance. An effective way to track student progress is to evaluate essential skill areas. Skill areas include those identified within a student's IEP goals and objectives. For example, an annual IEP goal for

63

Chapter Four
Reading
Intervention for
Students with
Learning
Disabilities

Part One
Foundations

a second-grade student with a disability in the area of reading may be as follows:

> After having one year of Direct Instruction in a small group, Carla will orally segment at least 40 phonemes correctly in one minute when given a phoneme segmentation fluency probe with two- to four-phoneme words.

Teachers should monitor progress weekly or at least every other week when working with students with disabilities; monitoring for students at risk for reading failure may occur less often (e.g., every other week, or monthly) (Shinn, Shinn, Hamilton & Clarke, 2002). The frequency of progress monitoring will depend on the specific skills and the severity of the deficit.

Strategy Instruction. Learning strategies help students with LD, and many with demonstrated learning problems become more effective learners (Clark, 2000). Such strategies include those techniques, rules, or principles that assist students to complete specific tasks independently (Friend & Bursuck, 2006). Using specific strategies during intervention helps teachers prompt students to remember important aspects of the instruction while gradually making students more responsible for their learning. Through strategy instruction, students learn new or difficult skills for the first time through directive and explicit guidance from teachers.

Research studies that include strategy instruction show better outcomes than those that do not (Clay, 1991; Deshler et al., 2001; Fletcher, Lyons, Fuchs & Barnes 2007; Friend & Bursuck, 2006; Palinscar & Brown, 1984; Pressley et al., 1992; Swanson & Hoskyn, 1998). Specifically, Swanson and Hoskyn (1998) conducted a meta-analysis of various methods of instruction, including with students with LD. After analyzing 180 studies, they concluded that strategy instruction demonstrated moderately strong effects on student outcomes. When coupled with methods of direction instruction, strategy instruction had significantly stronger positive effects on students' learning. Strategies assist students with short- and long-term memory deficits or with problems attending to tasks—common difficulties for children with disabilities (Haager & Klingner, 2005). Therefore, teachers should integrate strategy instruction in their reading intervention with students with LD.

Access to Core Reading and Language Arts Instruction

65

Chapter Four

Reading
Intervention for
Students with
Learning
Disabilities

Even when students with learning disabilities receive all or some of their reading and language arts instruction from a special education teacher, it is important for them to have access to the general education curriculum and grade-level standards. A great deal of rich vocabulary, comprehension, and critical-thinking experiences occur in the general education curriculum and reading/language arts instruction. By participating in the general education classroom for at least a portion of the school day, students with LD will have access to concepts, interactions, and thinking alongside their same-age, nondisabled peers. Students with LD will learn how to interact with both expository and narrative text through active participation in the general education language arts curriculum.

Students with LD served in pull-out settings often miss such experiences unless there is careful planning for their successful participation in general education classroom activities. Some ideas for ensuring students' access to important literacy experiences in the general education classroom include:

1. *Collaboration and planning.* It is important for the general and special education teachers to discuss the schedule, being mindful of opportune times for students to be present and engaged in meaningful read-alouds, literature experiences, and discussion of text.

2. *Peer support.* Paired learning activities can provide students with LD support from same-age nondisabled peers for engaging in follow-up activities focused on talking about text, writing about text, or participating in creative projects.

3. *Cooperative groups.* Students with LD receive support and encouragement for learning when group activities are carefully and heterogeneously structured, monitored, and supported to ensure that students can be successful. Carefully assigning group members' roles and having group guidelines will foster peer support for any students experiencing difficulty.

4. *Interactive writing activities.* When students are asked to write in response to literature or expository text, it reinforces students'

learning of key ideas and vocabulary. Additionally, interactive writing assignments allow the teacher to monitor students' understanding and to provide individual feedback and support.

5. *Modification of assignments.* General and special education teachers should work collaboratively to design appropriate accommodations for students with LD. Modifying the assignments, requiring fewer vocabulary words, reading aloud test instructions and/or items, and other adaptations provide necessary support and allow students to access important grade-level content.

Models of Reading Intervention

There are a number of service delivery models designed to meet the needs of students with disabilities during reading intervention. These services may be provided within the least restrictive environment (LRE) where students with disabilities receive services alongside nondisabled peers. Students with more severe reading deficits most often receive explicit reading instruction and support in more restrictive settings. Educators should familiarize themselves with these different models of service delivery and explore how reading intervention for students with LD and those at risk for reading failure may be provided. Table 4.3 summarizes the models most often encountered in schools and reviews the roles and responsibilities of general and special educators when providing reading intervention. Each model varies depending on where reading instruction is provided for students with LD, which students are included during reading intervention, and who provides intense reading intervention and support for students with LD.

Reading intervention for students with LD may occur within the general education classroom or in a separate classroom. This instruction may include only students with disabilities or a mixture of students with and without disabilities. Depending on the setting and service delivery model, the general and/or special education teacher may implement reading intervention for students with LD.

Regardless of the model being implemented, general and special educators should communicate regularly regarding the nature of the disability and how it specifically impacts the student's performance in the area of reading. How might the disability and processing deficit

TABLE 4.3 **Service Delivery Models for Students with Disabilities and At Risk Students**

Model	Setting	Students	Special Educator's Role	General Educator's Role
Inclusion	General education classroom setting for most if not all of instructional day	Students with disabilities and those at risk for reading failure	Provide explicit reading instruction for students with disabilities according to IEP goals in reading and those at risk for reading failure. Support students' progress on grade-level standards and curriculum in reading. Regularly monitor student progress in reading-related skills/goals and share with general educator and parents.[a]	Support students with disabilities and those at risk for reading failure during whole class and/or small group grade-level reading instruction. Provide necessary accommodations and modifications to grade-level reading curriculum, as indicated in IEP, for those with disabilities. Maintain samples of student work and share with special educator and parents.
Resource program (pull-out)	Special education classroom setting for a portion of instructional day	Students with disabilities	Provide explicit reading instruction according to IEP goals in reading. Provide exposure to grade-level standards and curriculum in reading. Regularly monitor student progress in reading-related skills/goals and share with general educator and parents.	Support students with disabilities during whole class and/or small group grade-level reading instruction when/if these students are present. Provide accommodations and modifications to grade-level curriculum. Maintain samples of student work and share with special educator and parents.

(continued)

TABLE 4.3 continued

Model	Setting	Students	Special Educator's Role	General Educator's Role
Self-contained classroom	Special education classroom for most if not all of instructional day	Students with disabilities	Provide explicit reading instruction according to IEP goals in reading. Provide exposure to grade-level standards and curriculum in reading. Regularly monitor student progress in reading-related skills/goals and share with parents.	Support students in academic areas not included as areas of need in IEP (e.g., physical education, music, art). Provide necessary accommodations and modifications as indicated in IEP. Maintain samples of student work and share with special educator and parents.
Learning center	General classroom for specific intervention instruction	Students with disabilities and those at risk for reading failure	Provide explicit reading instruction according to IEP goals in reading. Regularly monitor student progress in reading-related skills/goals and share with parents and general educators.[b]	Communicate grade-level standards and curriculum in reading and students' progress in reading to special educator, additional learning center instructors, and parents, as necessary.

[a]Students with very mild difficulties in reading may receive most of their reading instruction from a general education teacher while the special education teacher monitors students' progress.

[b]Special educators may or may not serve as coordinators of learning center models for individual school sites.

(e.g., auditory or visual processing disorder) affect reading performance, and how should the teacher take this into account during instruction? Teachers should discuss a student's present levels of performance and IEP goals and objectives related to reading. These may include goals to increase decoding or fluency levels and reading/listening comprehension. Teachers should agree on the specific method for monitoring progress toward IEP goals and objectives in reading (e.g., oral reading fluency probe) and how frequently these goals should be monitored (e.g., weekly, every other week). Therefore, communication among educators is critical, particularly when students can move regularly between classrooms and service providers.

69

Chapter Four
Reading
Intervention for
Students with
Learning
Disabilities

Summary

The reauthorization of the Individuals with Disabilities Education Act in 2004 allowed for the use of response to intervention as an alternative to the discrepancy approach for the purpose of identifying students with learning disabilities. This alternative requires general education teachers to implement effective core reading practices and scientific, research-based interventions for students experiencing difficulty in reading. Students no longer must wait until the later grades to receive necessary supports for their learning difficulties. Students' responsiveness to effective intervention instruction helps educators and school intervention teams determine whether or not a student's learning difficulties are a result of a true learning disability. Educators' use of progress-monitoring data is essential in supporting these decisions. Rather than depend solely on standardized assessment measures for determining special education eligibility, educational professionals now have measures and methods more reflective of classroom practices and performance-based standards.

Once identified for special education services, the content and methods of reading intervention for students with learning disabilities will vary depending on students' specific learning needs. However, regardless of age or grade, the content of instruction should reflect the essential beginning reading skills originally identified by the National Reading Panel in 2000, including instruction in phonemic (or phonological) awareness, phonics, fluency, comprehension, and vocabulary. Research on effective methods of reading intervention for students with LD reinforces several consistent practices, including ongoing progress monitoring, use of direct instruction methods, and strategy instruction, to name a few. Students may receive intervention and support from either a general and/or special educator, depending on the severity of the reading disability and the method of service delivery being implemented.

Changes in special education legislation promoting more inclusive experiences for students with LD make it necessary to prepare beginning and experienced teachers to support these students within general education classrooms. The instruction of students with LD must provide them with explicit intervention to address their individual reading needs and also support greater access to the general education reading/language arts curriculum. General and special educators should discuss the methods, cases, and research presented in this chapter and collaborate to better meet the needs of these students.

The authors would like to thank Clare Levy for all her research and work on this chapter.

Part Two

ERPI Implementation Guidelines

Part Two of this text provides the nuts and bolts of conducting early reading intervention. In Chapter 5, the scope and sequence of the Early Reading Project Intervention (ERPI) is presented. Chapter 5 gives a detailed description of phonological awareness (PA) and phonics—the content for explicit, systematic early reading interventions. It presents how to break down PA and phonics skills into teachable subskills for struggling readers. Chapter 6 explains the Core Intervention Model (CIM), the methods by which the ERPI is taught. The CIM is based on six principles of instruction: small groups, specific objectives, appropriate content, explicit and intense instruction, many opportunities for correct responses, and corrective feedback using the staircase approach. Chapter 7 presents how to incorporate the content and methods of intervention into a process for implementing and assessing intervention using data-based decision making. Data-based decision making gives teachers specific steps to take before, during, and after intervention for choosing students for intervention, planning intervention, and monitoring student progress. The final chapter, Chapter 8, provides the documents and activities—including schedules, data sheets, lesson plans, and so on—to guide teachers in implementing intervention in their own classroom.

To help describe the content and methods of the ERPI and the intervention process, we will follow two teachers and their students throughout Chapters 5 through 7. Ms. Perry's and Mr. Lee's students will provide examples of how ERPI can be used in a general education or a special education program.

Ms. Perry is a first-grade teacher at Lynn City Elementary School. She has been teaching first grade for seven years. She runs a well-organized classroom, with a warm and inviting demeanor. She greets the children with a smile each morning, and then they get to work. Her students come mostly from lower-socioeconomic families; about half of them are English learners. She has three languages represented in her classroom—English, Spanish, and Farsi (native language of Iran). During the day, Ms. Perry uses both small group and whole group instruction. She follows the state-adopted language arts curriculum, which is aligned with the state standards. Ms. Perry teaches in English only, but she does speak some Spanish. She is a very positive teacher and truly enjoys teaching. Ms. Perry's first-grade colleagues work well together, and they are discussing developing a intervention program for all first-graders based on Ms. Perry's current intervention program.

Two students from Ms. Perry's class are of particular interest. Yvonne and Ben are students who are struggling to learn to read. Yvonne is a vibrant, talkative girl. She speaks Spanish at home with her parents and younger siblings but English with her peers at school. Ms. Perry is concerned about Yvonne's progress in reading. She is making some progress but not as much as the other students. During whole group instruction, Yvonne offers answers, but they are generally incorrect. For example, Ms. Perry has the students tell her a funny made-up word that rhymes with *cup* before going to recess, Yvonne yells out "*Dog.*" Yvonne's seatwork is typically completed nicely, as she works closely with her friend, Isabel, who helps her with the activities. Yvonne's kindergarten teacher reported that she struggled learning her letter sounds in kindergarten and did not begin reading during the school year.

Ben is a monolingual English-speaking student who comes from a supportive and very involved family. His mother volunteers in the classroom each week. He gets along well with his peers and enjoys school, but Ms. Perry is beginning to see behavior difficulties during instruction. During whole class instruction, Ben is often bouncing up and down and has difficulty answering or following along with stories. He loves to sing and will join in when Ms. Perry plays music or allows the students to dance. During small group instruction, Ben struggles with learning how to blend letter sounds together. Ms. Perry has noted that he does not seem to hear all the sounds in spoken language. She has also discussed with his parents that he often forgets what he has learned from day to day.

Mr. Lee is a special education teacher. Mr. Lee has been teaching at Lynn City Elementary School for 20 years. He is well respected by his colleagues and collaborates with many teachers on campus. Mr. Lee has been running the learning center at Lynn City Elementary School for the last year and a half. Students both with and without disabilities come to the learning center Mondays, Wednesdays, and Fridays for extra support in reading and math. On Tuesdays and Thursdays, Mr. Lee is in the general education classrooms supporting students identified with disabilities in the core curriculum. He has been conducting reading interventions for years and is happy to have the opportunity to work with all struggling readers in the learning center.

Of special interest from Mr. Lee's caseload is Daniel. Daniel is a third-grade student with a learning disability. Mr. Lee began working with Daniel in the second grade when he came to the learning center for additional help in reading. Daniel struggled with school since kindergarten but was only identified as having a disability after having worked with Mr. Lee for a year. Daniel is a monolingual English-speaking student and a fabulous musician. He gets along well with his peers but gets frustrated easily with schoolwork that demands reading. Daniel's math skills are just below grade level. Mr. Lee has noticed that Daniel's anger and behavior difficulties are greatly reduced when he is having success with his schoolwork. Mr. Lee is confident that Daniel will become a better reader with the correct intervention.

CHAPTER 5

What Should I Teach?

The Scope and Sequence of Early Reading Interventions

Objectives

By the end of this chapter, the reader will be able to

1. Describe the content of phonological awareness instruction, including the following subskills: rime, onset, segmentation, and blending

2. Describe the content of phonics instruction, including letter-sound knowledge, decoding, and spelling

3. Support why teaching phonological awareness and phonics is necessary for struggling readers

4. Describe the scope and sequence of content needed in the Early Reading Project Intervention (ERPI)

A s discussed in Chapter 2, research-based reading instruction incorporates five critical components: phonological awareness, phonics (or alphabetic principle), fluency, vocabulary, and comprehension (National Reading Panel, 2000; see Figure 5.1). Early reading intervention includes two of these components: phonological awareness and phonics. These two components of reading are linked to the prevention of long-term reading difficulties. Both have a large

FIGURE 5.1   The Five Components of Reading Instruction

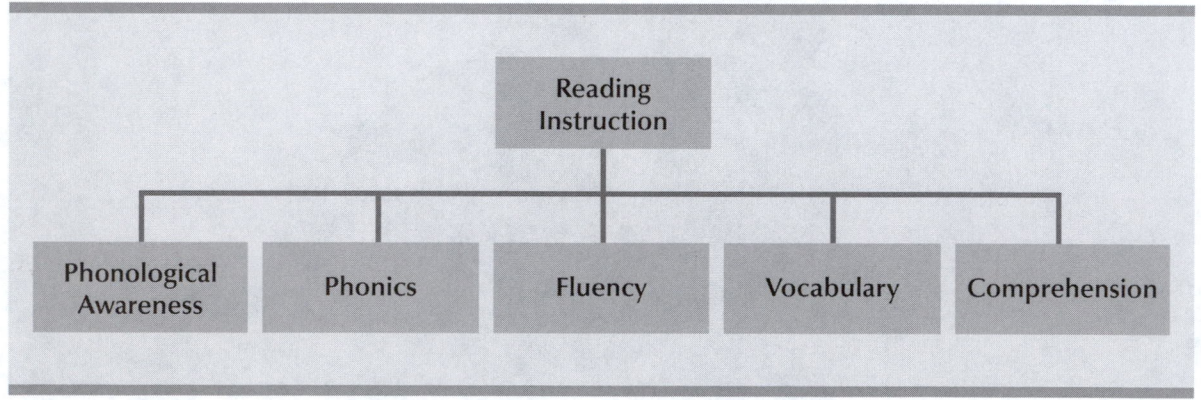

impact on students' ability to become proficient readers and are easily taught (Ehri, Nunes, Willows et al., 2001; Ehri, Nunes, Stahl & Willows, 2001). This chapter describes both phonological awareness and phonics skills and describes the scope and sequence of these skills in the Early Reading Project Intervention (ERPI)

The National Reading Panel (2000) describes phonemic awareness as one of the critical elements of reading instruction. Phonemic awareness is the understanding that words are made up of individual sounds or **phonemes**. In this book, the broader term *phonological awareness* (PA) is used. Phonological awareness is an umbrella term that includes phonemic awareness but also includes the understanding that words are parts of sentences, that syllables are parts of words, and that words are made up of sound parts (onset and rime). See Figure 5.2 for an illustration of each component of PA, with examples. Phonemic awareness is the most advanced skill under the phonological awareness "umbrella," and many times struggling readers, especially in early kindergarten and first grade, are not yet ready for instruction at the phoneme level. These students need to build other phonological awareness skills, such as rime and onset, to develop the foundational skills for phonemic awareness instruction.

FIGURE 5.2   Subskills of Phonological Awareness

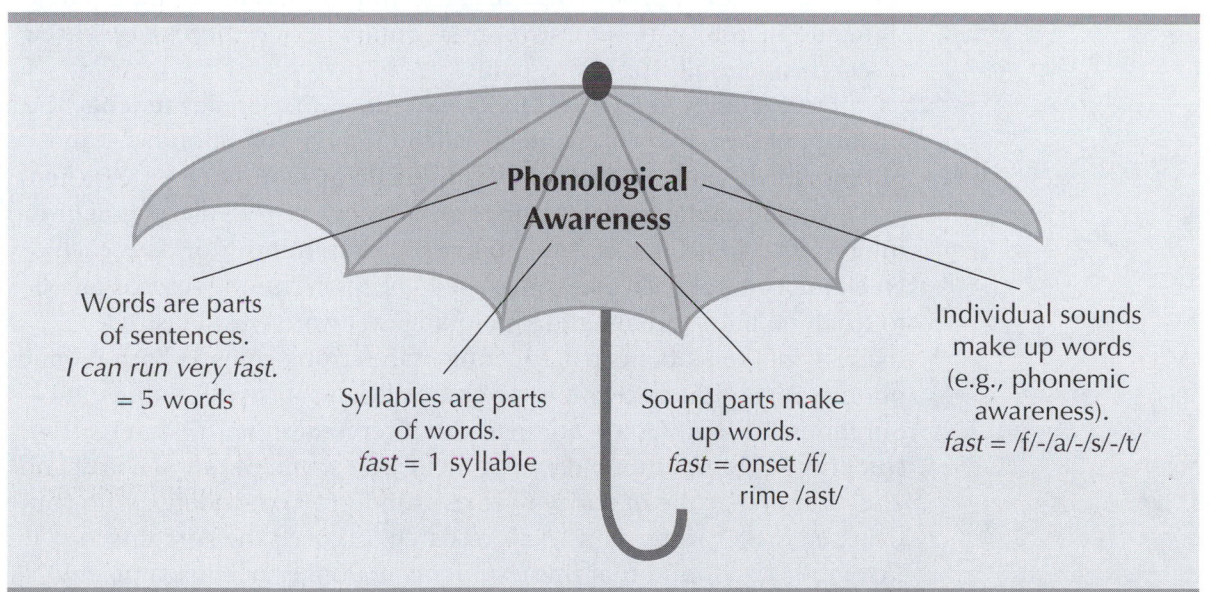

PA is an oral skill and requires the ability to understand that spoken language can be broken into parts. Phonics skills build on a student's PA skills by connecting the sounds heard to written letters and text. Phonics skills are often termed the *alphabetic principle*. The alphabetic principle involves understanding how written letters and sounds are connected (National Reading Panel, 2000). The alphabetic principle includes several subskills: letter-sound knowledge, sounding out words (decoding), and reading connected text (Simmons & Kame'enui, 1998).

Evidence for Providing Phonological Awareness and Phonics Interventions

Systematic, explicit interventions in phonological awareness (PA) and phonics are effective in remediating many early reading difficulties (Ehri, Nunes, Stahl et al., 2001; Ehri, Nunes, Willows et al., 2001; National Reading Panel, 2000). The majority of students respond to intervention in these areas, and skill deficits have been shown to ameliorate quickly. Generally, students in kindergarten and first grade who receive intervention in a small group for 20 to 30 minutes, three to five days a week will make adequate growth in these skills. As students move into second grade and beyond, they may not respond as well to intervention, and therefore more time in intervention may be necessary. Three research studies illustrate this point.

In two studies looking at kindergarten and first-grade students, the majority of students who were provided intervention in both PA and phonics made gains. In one study conducted by O'Conner (2007), first-grade students who were identified as at risk were provided small group intervention in groups of three to five for 30 minutes four days each week for 14 weeks. The activities used for intervention were designed to teach phonics and integrate phonological awareness skills. The majority of the students participating made strong gains in both PA and phonics. In another study, Coyne and colleagues (Coyne, Kame'enui, Simmons & Harn, 2004) conducted an intervention with kindergarten students for 30 minutes a day that included PA and phonics instruction. They found that the majority of at risk kindergarten students who participated made strong gains. This research followed the students into first grade and found that these students no longer needed supplemental intervention and were able to meet grade-level reading benchmarks with general classroom instruction.

In another study conducted with second-grade students, Vaughn and colleagues (Vaughn, Linan-Thompson & Hickman, 2003) found that intervention was effective but not as powerful as it was in the above studies with younger students. The researchers studied student response to supplemental instruction, which consisted of PA, phonics, and comprehension interventions for at risk second-grade students. After 10 weeks of supplemental instruction for 35 minutes daily, 10 of the 45 students met the grade-level benchmark criteria. Students who did not meet these criteria received 10 more weeks of modified intervention. After the second set of 10 weeks, 14 more students exited the intervention, and the other 21 students were provided a final round of 10 weeks of intervention. After 30 weeks of intervention, however, there were still 11 second-grade students who had not met grade-level benchmarks. Again, this indicates that earlier interventions are more powerful and that often older students will need more intervention to make growth.

The above research, along with a meta-analysis of research in the area (Ehri et al., 2001), indicates that PA intervention, coupled with intervention in letter-sound relationships (alphabetic principle), is more effective than oral PA intervention. Many students who have difficulty in PA make gains both in PA and word reading after receiving intervention (Brown & Felton, 1990; Torgesen & Davis, 1996; Foorman et al., 1997).

Interventions incorporating PA and phonics have been demonstrated to be effective for English learners as well (Gerber et al., 2004; Gunn, Biglan, Smolkowski & Ary, 2000; Leafstedt et al., 2004; Linan-Thompson , Vaughn, Hickman-Davis & Kouzekanani, 2003; Linan-Thompson et al., 2007; Richards et al., 2006). As reviewed in Chapter 3, PA is a skill that has cross-linguistic transfer, meaning that once students understand how to hear individual sounds in words, they can apply this skill to any language (Durgunoğlu et al., 1993). Crossover of PA has been shown in multiple languages, such as Turkish, Spanish, Chinese, and Japanese (Durgunoğlu, 2002). This implies that children from multiple language backgrounds can benefit from PA instruction regardless of the language being used to teach. Like the research on early intervention for monolingual students, the research on early intervention for ELs indicates that 20 to 30 minutes, three to five days a week will remediate skill deficits in PA.

Students with learning disabilities, even older students in third through fifth grade, can benefit from PA and phonics interventions (Torgesen et al., 2001). However, students identified with LD are typically one to two grade levels behind in reading, which means they need more time in intervention to develop necessary reading skills. Additionally, students with LD often have core phonological processing deficits (Stanovich & Siegel, 1994; Torgesen, 1999; Wagner & Torgesen, 1987). These deficits make it difficult for students with LD to process phonological information in oral and written form. Therefore, these students have difficulty learning early reading skills such as PA and phonics. For a student like Daniel, on Mr. Lee's caseload, intervention should be more frequent—five days a week and longer, 45 or more minutes each day. The intensity of the intervention needs to increase because Daniel is about two years behind his peers in reading and has major deficits in PA and phonics skills.

A student who is at risk but not identified with LD may have a deficit in one or two specific skill areas, respond to intervention, and learn to read on a typical timeline. In contrast, a student identified with LD will likely need continuous, intensive, and systematic intervention across multiple areas. Students with LD also need additional practice to achieve mastery as well as continuous review to maintain skill levels. For example, Daniel has participated in intervention to improve his PA skills and decoding of consonant-vowel-consonant (CVC) words, and he has become proficient in these skills. His teacher, Mr. Lee, has now begun to design intervention lessons teaching decoding of CVCC, CCVC, CCVCC, and CVCe (consonant-vowel-consonant-silent e) words. Mr. Lee also includes opportunities for continual practice of PA skills and decoding of CVC words in these lessons until mastery is demonstrated over time.

Struggling readers who have deficits in early reading skills benefit from systematic early reading intervention in PA and phonics. ELs can benefit from similar, if not the same, interventions as English speakers, and students with LD can make gains in PA and phonics when intervention is provided with more intensity and additional follow-up. Knowing this, teachers can follow a similar instructional scope and sequence during interventions for each of these groups of students. What then is the scope and sequence of early reading intervention that includes PA and phonics?

Scope and Sequence of the Early Reading Project Intervention

Intervention that combines both PA and phonics and is focused on the needs of each individual student is a key to developing successful readers and is the heart of the Early Reading Project Intervention (ERPI). PA and phonics both include subskills that, once understood, allow for easy modification of intervention. PA includes rime, onset, segmentation, and blending. Phonics includes both letter-sound relationships and decoding and spelling. The scope and sequence of ERPI is shown in Table 5.1. Moving down the scope and sequence, skills become more difficult and should be taught in the sequence listed. Moving across the scope and sequence, skills should be taught simultaneously. For example, students who are orally identifying words with the same beginning sound and words that rhyme are, at the same time, being introduced to letters and their corresponding sounds. Once students gain these initial skills, they move on to more difficult PA skills, such as segmenting and blending, while also beginning to spell and read basic CVC words. The goal of the intervention is for students to attain proficiency in reading and spelling through teaching a combination of PA and phonics skills. The next sections will describe this scope and sequence in more detail, first discussing PA and then phonics.

Phonological Awareness

For phonological awareness (PA) instruction, teachers use a two-level model of decision making for determining which PA skills to teach. For level 1, the teacher decides, based on assessment, which PA skill (i.e., rime, onset, segmentation, blending) the student needs and begins intervention with this element. For level 2, the teacher decides which type of task (i.e., identification, production, manipulation) should be used to teach the PA element. Both levels involve varying degrees of difficulty that allow for individualization during small group instruction.

Although there are multiple PA skills, typically, four are included in the ERPI and found most often in the research on PA interventions. These four skills include rime, onset, segmentation, and blending. **Rime** knowledge is the ability to identify rhyming words and to produce and manipulate the rime portion of the word—the part of the word or syllable that includes the vowel and the consonants that come

TABLE 5.1 Scope and Sequence of the Early Reading Project Intervention

Phonological Awareness *Rime/Onset/Blending/Segmentation*	Phonics *Letter-Sound Relationships*	Phonics *Decoding/Spelling*
1. Onset: Beginning sound identification		
2. Onset: Orally matching beginning sounds with pictures 3. Rime: Orally matching rhyming words with pictures	1. Letter-sound match	
4. Blending: Onset-rime blending orally 5. Segmenting: Onset-rime tap	↓	
6. Blending: 3-phoneme words orally 7. Segmenting: Tapping phonemes-three-phoneme words	2. Letter-sound flashcards	
8. Blending: 4- to 5-phoneme words 9. Onset: Producing a word that begins with the same beginning sound 10. Segmenting: Manipulating first letter in words orally		1. Spelling CVC words given the rime portion of the word (-at, spell *cat*) and reading the CVC words
11. Segmenting: Sound counting CVC words 12. Segmenting: Manipulating final sounds orally 13. Segmenting: Manipulating middle sounds orally 14. Rime: Producing a word that rhymes	↓	2. Spelling VC and CVC words and reading the words
		3. Manipulating sounds (first, final, or middle) to spell new CVC words to read 4. Reading CVC words in text
↓		5. Reading more difficult words[a] 6. Spelling more difficult words[a] 7. Manipulating sounds to spell more difficult words[a] 8. Reading more difficult words[a] in text

[a]More difficult words are all words that are taught after CVC words, including CVCC, CCVC, CCCVC, CVCe, CVVC, CCVVC, and so on, and also multisyllabic words.

Source: Leafstedt, Richards & Gerber, 2003.

after it. **Onset** knowledge is the ability to identify, produce, or manipulate the first sound(s) in a word. **Segmentation** is the ability to break up words into parts, whether onset-rime or individual phonemes. **Blending** is essentially the opposite skill of segmenting. It is the ability to hear the sounds in words (onset-rime or individual phonemes) and put the sounds together to make a word. Refer to Table 5.2 for definitions.

These PA skills develop in a fairly predictable sequence (Christensen, 1997; Leafstedt, 2003). First, students are able to identify words that have the same rime—that is, words that rhyme or sound the same. At this time, students also begin to identify words that have the same beginning sound, or onset. Following this, students begin to understand that words are made up of individual sounds, or segments, and that the sounds can be put together, or blended, to make a word.

Each of the PA skills (onset, rime, segmentation, and blending) can be taught through the various tasks (identification, production, and manipulation). Figure 5.3 shows the progression of difficulty for each

TABLE 5.2 Definitions of the Four Elements of Phonological Awareness

PA Element	Definition
Rime c<u>ap</u>, bl<u>ack</u>	Identifying, producing, or manipulating the ending sound in a word (includes the vowel and all consonants after it)
Onset <u>c</u>ap, <u>bl</u>ack	Identifying, producing, or manipulating the beginning sound in a word (includes the consonants before the first vowel)
Segmentation cap = c-ap or c-a-p black = bl-ack or b-l-a-ck	Breaking up words into smaller parts, whether onset-rime or individual phonemes
Blending c-ap and c-a-p = cap bl-ack and b-l-a-ck = black	Putting together the sounds in words together, whether onset-rime or individual phonemes

element. Identification is the easiest task and only requires a student to respond by telling the word or choosing a picture that has a given sound. Production is the next most difficult task. When doing production tasks, the teacher asks the students to come up with the words or sounds on their own. For example, a teacher would say, "Tell me a word that rhymes with *cat*." Manipulation is the most difficult task. In a manipulation task, the student is expected to change sounds in a word to make new words. For example, the teacher would ask, "If you take off the /l/ in *log* and add a /d/ to the beginning, what word do you make?"

Table 5.3 provides examples of how each skill can be taught using the relevant tasks. By using the skills and tasks, a teacher is able to design an intervention to meet specific student needs. For example, if there is a small group of students in a class who all need to work on rime but all are not ready to work on production of rhyming words, a teacher can easily **differentiate** the instruction for individual students within this small group. One student can be working on rime identification while another is working on rime production. By changing the question from "Which word rhymes with *cat, bat,* or *log*" to "Tell me a word that rhymes with *cat*," individual student needs can be addressed.

**FIGURE 5.3   Progression of PA Tasks and Skills,
from Easiest to Most Difficult**

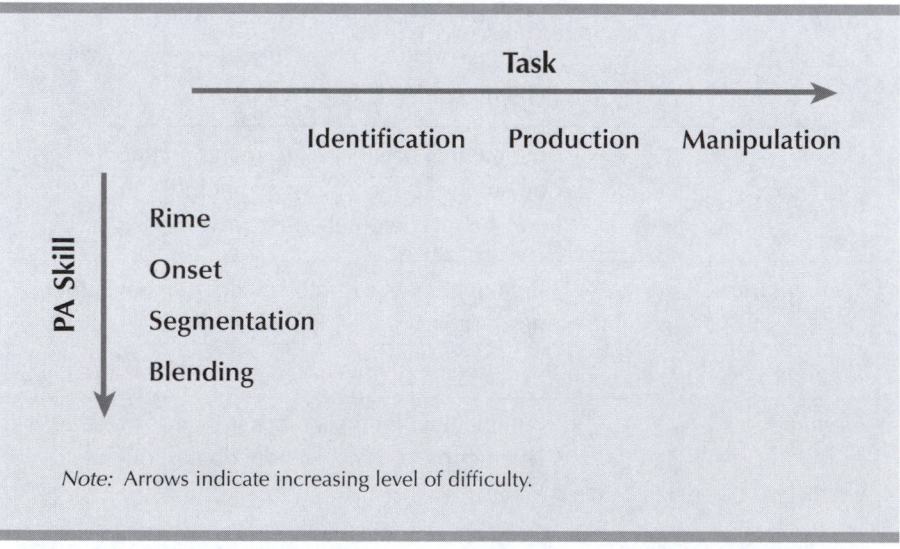

Note: Arrows indicate increasing level of difficulty.

The developmental sequence and features of PA instruction are the same for ELs struggling to learn to read in English as they are for English speakers (Chiappe, Siegel & Wade-Wooley, 2003; Leafstedt, 2003; Linan-Thompson et al., 2003). This said, the instructional strategies that are effective with ELs—additional modeling and visuals to enhance understanding—need to be used in intervention as well (refer to Chapter 3). For ELs like Yvonne, Ms. Perry follows the sequence of PA activities in Table 5.1, beginning with rime and onset activities and moving to segmenting and blending. When Ms. Perry plans for intervention for Yvonne, she supports the activities with pictures. For example, Ms. Perry did an onset-rime blending activity (e.g., "What word am I saying? /b/-/at/") with Yvonne's intervention group. After the students got the correct answer, Ms. Perry showed a picture of a bat. Ms. Perry also provides additional modeling for Yvonne and provides the directions in

TABLE 5.3   Examples of Identification, Production, and Manipulation Tasks for Each of the PA Skills

PA Skill	Identification Example	Production Example	Manipulation Example
Rime cap, black	Which word rhymes, or sounds the same as, *cap*? *Rap* or *snail*?	Tell me a word that rhymes with *cap*.	What sounds do you change in *cap* to make *cut*?
Onset cap, black	Which two words have the same beginning sound? *Cap, come, snail*?	Tell me the first sound in *cap*. Tell me a word that starts with the same sound as *cap*.	Put a /c/ at the beginning of /ap/. What word does it make?
Segmentation cap = c-a-p black = b-l-a-ck		Tell me the two parts you hear in *cap*. Tell me all the sounds in *black*.	What sounds do you change in *flap* to make *flop*?
Blending c-a-p = cap b-l-a-ck = black		What word do the sounds /c/-/ap/ make? What word do these sounds make: /b/-/l/-/a/-/ck/?	

clear, simplistic terms. At times, Ms. Perry explains the task in Spanish to ensure that Yvonne understands the task. In order to benefit from intervention, the students must understand how to engage in the tasks, but since PA has cross-linguistic transfer, the students do not need to have a deep understanding of the words used for the PA activities. Therefore, PA can be taught even before the student has developed English proficiency. For example, in the onset-rime blending activity above, Ms. Perry makes sure that Yvonne understands that she needs to put the sounds together to make a word, but Ms. Perry knows that Yvonne does not need to understand what each word used in the activity means (i.e., *bat, lake, box,* etc.) to do the task. This is not to imply that Yvonne does not need instruction in vocabulary or comprehension skills. English language development should be taught during the day; however, it is important to keep the intervention focused on the specific goals and objectives set for each student.

Students with LD also follow this same developmental sequence of PA skills; however, the rate of development is often slower. Since many students identified with LD in reading have core phonological processing deficits due to the nature of their disability (Wagner & Torgesen, 1987), these students need more intensive and specific focus on these skills during intervention. For example, before receiving intervention, Daniel "shut down" and refused to engage during classroom phonics instruction. This was likely due to the fact that the instruction was too difficult and not broken down to meet his specific needs. Despite the fact he is in third grade, Daniel still needs intervention in PA skills, specifically segmentation and blending, to support his phonics skills. Mr. Lee adapts the intervention to use more age-appropriate materials. For example, in kindergarten, blending the sounds in words like *slide* and *frog* are appropriate, but Mr. Lee chooses words such as *soccer* and *alien* for older students. Because Daniel is an older student and at least one grade level behind his peers, the pacing of instruction should be adapted as well. Mr. Lee aims at keeping a rapid teaching pace so that Daniel can meet objectives quickly.

Phonics

Phonics instruction is defined as instruction that teaches students the alphabetic principle—the relationships between written letters and spoken sounds (CIERA, 2003). Teaching phonics with PA skills is particularly important when teaching more sophisticated skills such as segmenting and blending. Examples of activities that integrate PA and phonics are shown in Figure 5.4. In the first activity, students segment three-phoneme words (i.e., *cat, bit, fun*) by tapping the three sounds of the words on colored placeholders. In the second activity, students put letter tiles (or you can use post-its) on the placeholders to spell the words and then again tap the sounds. Practice in segmenting the words orally and then using letter tiles to segment words into individual sounds provides students with the needed practice and connection between sounds and letters (Ehri et al., 2001). Once students are able to orally break words apart and put them back together, they can add their knowledge of letters and begin to read and spell words.

As with PA instruction, phonics instruction (teaching the alphabetic principle) is best understood by examining the subskills: letter-sound correspondences, decoding, and reading connected text (Simmons & Kame'enui, 1998). Letter-sound correspondences are the specific letter-sound relationships for the individual letters of the alphabet as well as

FIGURE 5.4 **Lesson Combining PA and Phonics for First-Grade Intervention**

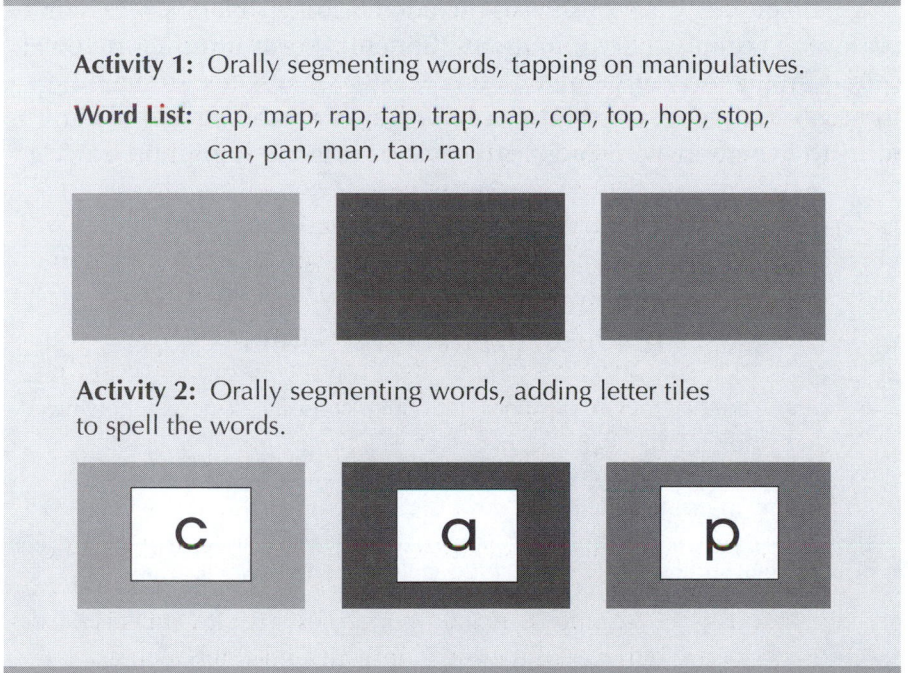

Activity 1: Orally segmenting words, tapping on manipulatives.

Word List: cap, map, rap, tap, trap, nap, cop, top, hop, stop, can, pan, man, tan, ran

Activity 2: Orally segmenting words, adding letter tiles to spell the words.

c a p

consonant and vowel blends (i.e., sh, bl, ou, ea). Letter-sound relationships should be taught in a logical sequence, considering frequency of use and usability with other known letters. One suggested order (from Carnine et al., 2004) is shown in Table 5.4. Initially, when teaching letters and sounds, teachers should introduce three to four consonants and one vowel at a time. This allows students to begin reading and spelling actual words.

For students like Yvonne, who are developing letter-sound knowledge and PA skills, teachers can incorporate phonics and PA skills in intervention by focusing on the onset portion of the word. For example, Ms. Perry asks Yvonne, "What sounds do you hear in *cat*? Yvonne responds orally, "/C/-/at/." Then Ms. Perry asks her to identify the letter tile that corresponds with the beginning sound. For students who are ready to segment and blend words and who have learned letter-sound relationships, teachers can design interventions that focus on segmenting and blending skills as well as beginning decoding and spelling with CVC words. For example, later in intervention, Ms. Perry asks Yvonne, "What are all the sounds you hear in *cat*?" She responds, "/C/-/a/-/t/." Then Ms. Perry has her spell the word and then read the word she spelled.

The scope and sequence of phonics instruction after teaching initial letter(s)-sound(s) relationships is included below in Table 5.5. It is important to begin with two- to three-phoneme words using short vowel sounds in the form of VC and CVC (i.e., *at, fog, lip*). Once students master VC and CVC words, they can move on to reading and spelling four- to five-phoneme words with consonant blends and short vowels.

TABLE 5.4.   Recommended Order for Introducing Letters and Sounds

1. Choose three to four consonants. (Introduce consonants in the following order: m, s, t, f, d, r, g, l, h, c, b, n, k, v, w, j, p, y, x, q, z.)

2. Choose one vowel. (Introduce vowels in following order: a, i, o, u, e.)

3. Continue adding two to three consonants and one vowel at a time as students master previous letters.

Source: This recommended order is taken from Carnine, Silbert, Kame'enui & Tarver, 2004.

Following this, instruction focuses on reading and spelling words with long vowels and the silent *e*. Finally, instruction on vowel blends, more difficult consonant blends, and multisyllabic words can take place.

For ELs who are struggling to read, the same scope and sequence of phonics instruction is used as for English speakers. However, some letter sounds may be more difficult for students who speak another

TABLE 5.5 Scope and Sequence of Teaching Phonics beyond Letter-Sound Relationships

Target Skill	Example	Practice with Text
Two- to three-phoneme words with short vowel sounds	at bat map rap	• Reading and spelling words (using word families) • Short sentences
Four- to five-phoneme words with consonant blends and short vowels	flat brat clap strap	• Reading and spelling words (using word families) • Short sentences
Three-phoneme words with long vowels and silent *e*	cane, plane, mane cute, flute, mute	• Reading and spelling words (using word families and discrimination of short and long vowels, i.e., *cane—can, cute—cut*) • Reading sentences and short passages
Three- to five-phoneme words with vowel combinations	bead crawl group streak	• Reading and spelling words • Reading sentences and short passages
Multisyllabic words	un-der-stand be-fore re-mem-ber cel-e-brate	• Reading and spelling words • Reading sentences and short passages

language. For example, Yvonne, whose first language is Spanish, has a very difficult time differentiating vowel sounds. Often, when she is shown the letter *i*, she will tell the sound for the long vowel *e*. This makes sense, given that in Spanish the letter *i* makes the long *e* sound. For ELs, these difficulties will differ depending on the student's native language and exposure to English.

For students with LD, again the same scope and sequence is followed for phonics as for all learners. The core phonological deficits that affect the PA skills of students with LD also affect their phonics skills. Therefore, it is likely that these students will need interventions that are more intensive, longer in duration, and more frequent to achieve growth in these skills. For example, Daniel is not yet ready for instruction in multisyllabic words, which is the instruction currently taking place in his classroom. During intervention, Mr. Lee will focus on more basic phonics skills, such as single-syllable words with short and long vowels, in order to provide Daniel with the necessary foundational skills and to allow him to experience success with the skills. An intervention designed to meet Daniel's needs will provide him with the necessary prerequisite skills and the motivation to learn.

Summary

Two of the five components of reading recognized by the National Reading Panel—phonological awareness (PA) and phonics—are key elements of early reading intervention. A plethora of research has demonstrated that the scope and sequence of early reading intervention must include both PA and phonics skills. This is true for all struggling readers, including students who are English learners and those who have a learning disability. Both PA and phonics should be taught in a systematic manner. PA skills should be taught in a developmental sequence, taking into consideration the difficulty of the PA element and instructional task. Phonics instruction should move from letter-sound relationships to decoding words and then to incorporating connected text.

How Should I Teach It?

Intervention Methods and
Teaching Strategies

Objectives

By the end of this chapter, the reader will be able to

1. Describe the six principles of the Core Intervention Model

2. Write clear intervention lesson objectives

3. Write a lesson plan that includes activities that break down PA and phonics skills for students

4. Develop staircase procedures for corrective feedback

Now that the scope and sequence of early reading intervention has been presented, let's examine how these skills should be taught to meet individual learners' needs in a classroom with many individual differences. This chapter focuses on the methods of teaching that are best suited for teaching early reading skills to struggling readers.

The Core Intervention Model of Instruction

The **Core Intervention Model** (CIM) (Gerber et al., 2004) is presented as a model for providing intervention. The CIM has been effective in remediating early reading difficulties in struggling readers, including English learners and those at risk for reading disabilities (Filippini, 2008; Gerber et al., 2004; Leafstedt et al., 2004; Richards et al., 2006; Solari & Gerber, 2008). The CIM is an instructional model based on theories of direct instruction. The research on direct instruction as a method for improving the academic success of low-performing students is vast (see Chapters 2 and 4). Similar to direct instruction, the six principles of CIM are that (1) students are taught in a small group; (2) specific objectives are set; (3) content and materials are appropriate for students' ability level; (4) skills are taught intensively, explicitly, and at a rapid pace; (5) students are provided opportunities for many correct responses; and (6) explicit correction procedures are used. In the following sections, each of the six principles of the Core Intervention Model will be described.

Principle 1. Teach in a small group.

In order for struggling readers to benefit, the CIM needs to be conducted in small groups. Over the years, research has demonstrated that small groups allow teachers to focus more on individual learning needs and to give students more attention than they would receive in whole class grouping (Elbaum et al., 1999). Small groups have been defined as 10 or fewer. However, reading research investigating various groupings of students has suggested that students make the most gains in small groups of three to four students (Elbaum, Vaughn & Hughes, 1999). In larger groups, even those with only seven students, teachers have more difficulty meeting student needs, and students do not have as many opportunities to respond. Likewise, one-to-one instruction has not been demonstrated to have more impact on student growth than small group

Box 6.1

Amount of Intervention Needed

How many minutes per day and how many days per week should students be provided early reading intervention?

The answer to this question will vary depending on the needs and grade level of the student. Research shows that at minimum, the intervention must take place at least 30 minutes a week for 10 weeks to achieve results (Ehri et al., 2001). However, for students who are very low performing, more intervention is necessary, generally for 20 to 30 minutes, three to five days a week for 10 weeks (O'Connor, 2007; Leafstedt et al., 2004). (For kindergartners, 15 minutes may be more realistic.) For students who already have an identified learning disability, generally 45 or more minutes of intervention five days a week for more than 10 weeks is necessary (Vaughn & Roberts, 2007). For students with learning disabilities, especially older students, part of intervention should be devoted to early skills, with the additional time used to develop more complex reading skills, such as fluency, vocabulary, and comprehension.

instruction, particularly for early reading skills, as students also learn from each other (Ehri et al., 2001). To maximize the impact of intervention, three to four students is the optimal size for a small group. This number allows students to have a great number of opportunities to respond and also allows them to observe their peers responding correctly, thereby serving as a model. When delivering intervention in small groups, the length of intervention will vary with individual student needs (see Box 6.1).

Principle 2. Set specific objectives.

Intervention is designed to target individual student needs based on assessment data and teacher observation. Goals for each student are set for the intervention, and specific daily **objectives** are set for each lesson. Objectives are based on **target skills** and should follow the developmental scope and sequence of acquiring early reading skills. (See scope and sequence in Chapter 5.) In order to have meaningful objectives for intervention, they must be observable and measurable. This means that the teacher needs to observe the student doing the behavior and then be able to determine if the student has met the objective. Table 6.1 includes examples of both initial and final objectives written by Ms. Perry after applying the observable, measurable criteria.

TABLE 6.1   Initial and Final Objectives for Intervention

Initial Objectives	Final Objectives
1. Students will know how to blend words.	1. Students will orally blend CVC words with short /a/ and /o/ sounds.
2. Students will understand how to segment four-phoneme words.	2. Students will segment words with beginning consonant blends (CCVC words).
3. Students will practice spelling.	3. Students will spell CVC words ending in -/at/.

In example 1, Ms. Perry initially wrote, "Students will know how to blend words." Can she observe this? No, she cannot see if the students "know" how to blend; she can only see what the students actually do. Can she measure this? No, it is not clear what the type of words or sounds are or how the student is supposed to demonstrate blending. After collaborating with her first-grade team, Ms. Perry rewrote the objective to read, "Students will orally blend CVC words with short /a/ and /o/ sounds." Can she observe the students doing this behavior? Yes, she can hear the students orally blending CVC words. Will she be able to measure this? Yes, she can ask the students to blend words with these sounds to determine if they have met the objective.

Before starting the activities in the intervention, students need to be told the objective in "student-friendly" language. An example of this language is, "Today we are going to be learning how to put sounds together to make words. All the words will have the /a/ and /o/ sounds in them." This explanation aids in making the intervention explicit to students and lets them know what they are expected to accomplish by the end of the intervention lesson.

Principle 3. Choose content and materials appropriate for each student's ability.

In planning for intervention, the content and materials selected must be appropriate for each individual student's ability. Content and materials should specifically target the student's individual needs. Sometimes this will mean that individual students in the group may require different content and materials even though they are working toward the same objective and are participating in the same activities. An example is shown in Figure 6.1. In this group of four students, all students are working toward the same objective—spelling and reading CVC words. Three of the students, including Yvonne, are reading and spelling CVC words on post-it squares and can produce all three sounds/letters. Ben is also reading and spelling CVC words, but since he is not ready to produce all three sounds/letters, he is provided the rime portion of the word on a large post-it and only adds the first sound/letter with a smaller post-it.

Selecting examples for the activities must also be appropriate for each lesson and individual student. If, during an intervention lesson, the objective is for students to read and spell CVC words and Ms. Perry

**FIGURE 6.1 Modifying Content and Materials
to individual Needs**

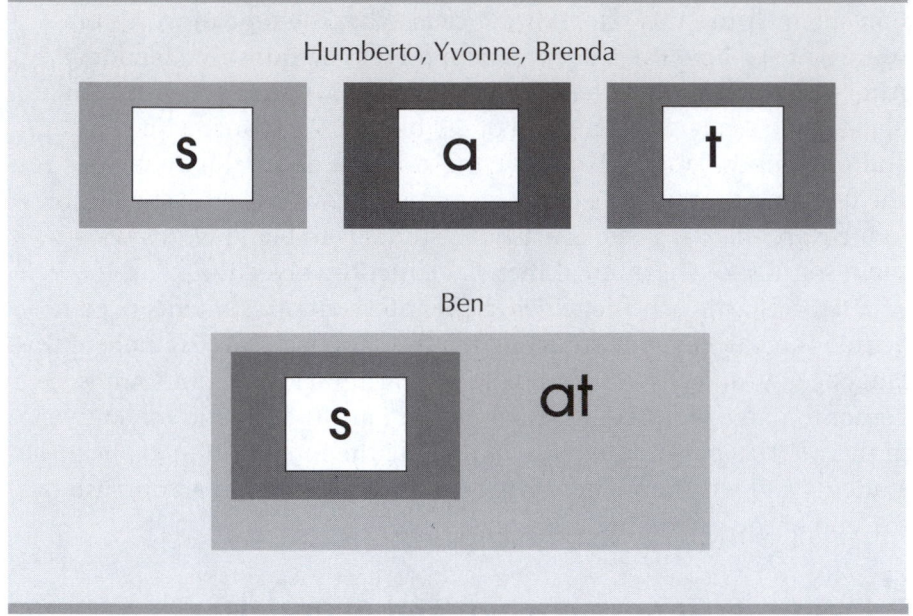

has only reviewed the letters/sounds *a, m, s, i, t, f, d, r, o,* and *g,* then the words chosen for the lesson should only include words that can be made with these letters/sounds. Table 6.2 contains a list of words that can be used to meet the objective using only the letters/sounds above. In this case, the letter *e* has not been reviewed, and therefore the word *peg* would not be an appropriate word to use for this lesson.

**TABLE 6.2 Word List for Reading
and Spelling CVC Words**

Sample word list for lesson with letters/sounds *a, o, t, d, g, m, f, s, r*			
-at	-ot	-ad	-og
mat, fat, sat, rat	tot, dot, rot, got	mad, sad, dad, rad	fog, dog

Principle 4. Teach skills explicitly, intensively, and at a rapid pace.

Teaching explicitly involves several techniques: modeling, breaking tasks and skills into steps, and providing guided and independent practice. First, explicit teaching involves **modeling** the activity by telling and showing the students what they are going to do. In most cases, while modeling the activity, teachers are also modeling their thinking as they are doing the tasks in a "think-aloud." This approach demonstrates to students the strategies that good readers use. For example, when doing an activity in which students have to produce a word with the same onset, or beginning sound, as another word, using the following language will help students develop a strategy for this task:

> I want to think of a word that starts with the same sound as *man*. (*Use picture for EL support.*) *Man, m-an*, I hear the /m/ sound at the beginning. What is another word I can think of that starts with the /m/ sound? Hmmm . . . *mouse*, starts with the /m/ sound. *Man, mouse*—I hear the /m/ sound in both of the words. (*Write the words on the board.*) *Man, mouse*—those both start with the same letter *m*. (*Underline the* m *in both words.*)

For many average-achieving students, these strategies are learned without explicit instruction, but for struggling readers, strategies will not be learned unless they are explicitly taught. (Refer to Chapter 4 for more detail regarding strategy instruction.)

Second, explicit teaching requires that tasks and skills be broken down into steps. If there are several steps to complete the task, they must be broken down so that the students can be successful. For example, if the objective for Yvonne's group is for the students to read and spell CVC words with short /a/ and /o/ sounds, there are several steps that need to occur for this to happen:

1. Students must know the letter-sound relationships for /a/ and /o/.

2. Students must know the consonant sounds to be used to make the words.

3. Students must be able to segment and blend sounds.

When designing a lesson to meet this objective, Ms. Perry includes activities that provide students the needed support to perform this task successfully. A sample lesson that breaks down these skills is shown in Figure 6.2. This lesson includes an activity that reviews the letters/ sounds that will be used in the lesson, an activity that involves segmenting words orally through sound counting, an activity that includes blending words orally, and finally an activity that involves reading and spelling CVC words. The first three activities take only a few minutes each and are included to review the key skills needed to meet the intervention lesson objective—reading and spelling CVC words.

Third, explicit instruction involves providing **guided practice—** opportunities for practice with the teacher—followed by **independent practice**. Guided practice is a key step in providing the student practice with assistance. After Ms. Perry models the task, she then does several examples with the students. After providing students the opportunity to practice with assistance, they are given several opportunities to practice independently. Included in independent practice is continuous review of previously taught skills. Independent practice and continuous review assist struggling readers to master the skills being taught. Unlike general classroom reading instruction, which often requires that a teacher move on to the next skill before all students have mastered it, intervention is focused on targeting specific skills that students need until they have mastered those skills. Daniel, the student with LD on Mr. Lee's caseload, needs to continue to practice after he has learned a skill in order to maintain his mastery of that skill and to enable generalization beyond reading during intervention time. On Monday, Mr. Lee taught a lesson on spelling CCVC words (e.g., *flat)*. He will continue to teach this skill for the rest of the week or until the students have demonstrated mastery of the skill on weekly assessments. Although he will move on to spelling CVCC words (e.g., *fast)* the next week, he will review CCVC words at the beginning of these lessons. This will allow for additional practice and review of the mastered skill.

Intensive intervention includes three elements: group size, additional time, and pacing. To provide students intensive intervention, group size must be small, and students must have adequate time, in addition to general classroom instruction, dedicated to intervention— namely, 20 to 30 minutes three to five days each week. To increase the intensity of intervention, the teacher can make the group smaller or add additional time (Vaughn et al., 2007). Intensive intervention also

FIGURE 6.2   Lesson Plan Showing Breakdown of Skills

Lesson Plan

Date: 1/30 **Lesson number:** 8 **Group:** 1 **Students present:** Yvonne, Ben, Brenda, Humberto	**Materials:** Letter cards Grab bag, with picture cards Post-its Index cards **Minutes of instruction:** 20

Objective: The students will read CVC words and spell CVC words using the word families -at, -ad, -ot, -og (Tell students the objective in student-friendly language.)

Reviewed skills: Letter sounds, segmenting three-phoneme words using fingers to count sounds, orally blending three- to four-phoneme words

Word Families

-at	-ad	-ot	-og
mat, fat, sat, rat	mad, sad, dad, rad	tot, dot, rot, got	fog, dog

Lesson

Activity 1 (**2 minutes**)—Letter-sound review
Show letter card; have students say letter sound and name (*a, o, t, d, g, m, f, s, r*)

Activity 2 (**3 minutes**)—Review of blending
Grab bag–Guess-My-Word blending activity using three- or four-phoneme words

Pull picture card from bag. Do not show students picture. Segment the word. Students blend the sounds to guess the word. Once students correctly blend the word, show the picture.

Activity 3 (**3 minutes**)—Review of finger-counting number of sounds
Say a word (*mat*). Students segment the word using fingers to show how many sounds the word has. Have students tell how many sounds.

Activity 4 (**12 minutes**)—Reading and spelling CVC words
Pass out post-its, index cards, and pencils.

Model: "Today we are going to use our segmenting and blending skills to read and spell words. I am going to show you what we are going to do. I want to spell the word *sat.*" (Segment with finger counting.) "/S/-/a/-/t/. That is three sounds. I will put out three post-its. First, I hear /s/. Let me think what letter makes /s/. *S*—that is the first letter. Second, I hear /a/. I know *a* makes /a/. Last I hear /t/. *T* makes /t/." (As I say this, write the letter on the post-it.) "Let me read it—*sat.* That is right. Now I will write it on my index card and practice reading it."

Guided Practice: "Let's do some together." Do four to five examples with the students using the same language. Use the word families to choose words.

Independent Practice: Have students do four to five words on their own while you provide feedback.

needs to be conducted at a rapid pace. This does not mean to just "go fast." It means that the pace of the lessons needs to move quickly. This may seem contrary to what many would think, but rapid pacing is critical, because students who are struggling readers have fallen behind their peers, which means that they need to learn much more in a shorter amount of time to get back on track (Engelman et al., 1988). Rapid pace also keeps students' attention. If students constantly need to respond, there is less time for distraction or inattention, which tends to occur more often with struggling readers. To ensure rapid pacing, the teacher must control the instruction by knowing exactly what the goals and objectives are, modeling examples while keeping teacher talk to a minimum, and exhibiting a high level of enthusiasm to hold student attention.

Principle 5. Provide students with opportunities for many correct responses.

During intervention, it is important to maximize the number of correct response opportunities for each student. Research has shown that the more responses students give, the more growth they make (see Box 6.2). Struggling readers, particularly in a whole group setting, either do not take the risk to respond or, when they do respond, often are incorrect. Therefore, during intervention, struggling readers need to have many opportunities to respond correctly. Using the principles of the CIM already described (i.e., stating the objective, breaking down the skills, having appropriate content and materials, and providing explicit and intensive teaching), teachers create a learning environment in which students are participating in tasks targeted to their individual needs and have more opportunities for responding correctly.

To maximize the number of student responses, Ms. Perry provides opportunities for students to respond in a variety of ways. She uses both choral, or unison, responses as well as individual opportunities for students to respond. Choral response allows her to increase the number of responses possible during a given intervention lesson in a small group setting. Additionally, individual responses are needed to determine if a student has acquired the skill being taught. For students who appear to be only imitating others in the group or are not responding during the choral responses, individual responding allows the teacher

Box 6.2

101

Chapter Six
How Should I
Teach It?

Student Responses and Growth

In a research study investigating four low-performing students (Richards, Leafstedt & Gerber, 2006), students who showed the most growth during intervention were also those who made the greatest number of responses during intervention. Although this research does not indicate a "magic" number of responses, students who averaged over three responses per minute were most successful.

Students who achieved the most growth responded during group choral responses and individual responses but also mouthed the words or formed words when it was another student's turn. The study indicated that all students had equal opportunities to respond. Students who did not achieve growth tended not to respond during choral responses or when it was another student's turn. For these students, it is likely that more opportunities for individual responses are necessary.

to give these students more response opportunities and practice. However, it is important not to discount imitating, as it leads to learning by providing additional practice and keeping students engaged with the learning activity. Ms. Perry also provides opportunities for students to respond either orally, in writing, or by demonstrating through the use of manipulatives. During a given intervention lesson, it benefits students if they have various ways in which to respond. One reason is that it helps to hold student attention during the intervention; another is that some students may be more motivated to respond in one way than another. A few of the students in Ms. Perry's intervention group are English learners, such as Yvonne. Ms. Perry knows that these students may not feel as comfortable responding orally and do not always participate fully in these activities. Therefore, she follows an activity done orally with an activity in which students use manipulatives to respond. For example, the first activity Ms. Perry does in the intervention lesson is orally blending four- and five-phoneme words. The second activity she does is spelling CVC words. In this activity, the students use letter tiles to spell words.

As students respond correctly, Ms. Perry praises the students abundantly, making their correct response a "big deal." This reinforcement is useful for maintaining attention, but more important, when Ms. Perry praises a student's response, the student is more likely to respond again. She uses praise that is deliberate and systematic. In a spelling activity, Yvonne correctly spelled the word *cut* after she segmented the sounds in the word and counted them on her fingers. Ms. Perry praised her by saying, "Great job, Yvonne. That's right, *cut* is spelled *c-u-t*. I like how you counted the sounds on your fingers to help you spell the word." For students who are low performing, praise is an essential part of intervention. These students often do not receive praise during whole group instruction, since they often do not take the risk to respond or, if they do respond, are often incorrect. During intervention, incorrect responses should be ignored. It is difficult, but teachers should resist the temptation to say, "No, that is not correct" or call on another student to provide the correct response. In the next section, the specific correction procedures are outlined in which teachers lead students to the correct answer.

Principle 6. Provide corrective feedback using the staircase approach.

Correction procedures are a critical component of direct instruction models of teaching. In the Core Intervention Model, explicit correction procedures are the crux of the model. Students are praised for correct responses. When an incorrect answer is given, students are led to the correct answer while the incorrect response is ignored. After an incorrect response, students are provided the opportunity to respond immediately to a simplified question or task. Correction procedures involve using the **correction staircase** to correct students during instruction. The staircase approach ensures that students are led to the correct answer and given the opportunity to respond independently to the original task.

To use the staircase approach, objectives must be clearly stated and understood. The teacher must break the objective into steps that will lead the student to the correct answer. If a student is not able to respond to the task, the teacher takes the student down the staircase to an easier task. When the student can respond independently, the

Lesson objective: Students will tell a word that rhymes with a given word.

Step 1: Original question: "What is a word that rhymes with *frog*?"

Step 2: Yes/no question: "Does *log* rhyme with *frog*?"

Step 3: Telling the answer: "*Log* rhymes with *frog*. What rhymes with *frog*?"

Step 4: Say and have the student repeat: Say, "*Log*. Good. *Log* rhymes with *frog*."

teacher takes the student back up the staircase until he or she is able to complete the original task. In the example in Figure 6.3, the original task (step 1) is "What is a word that rhymes with *frog*?" If the student does not respond correctly, the teacher moves down the staircase to the easier yes/no question (step 2)—"Does *log* rhyme with *frog*?" If the student still does not get the correct answer, the next step is taken—imitation/modeling (step 3)—"*Log* rhymes with *frog*. What rhymes with *frog*?" Again, if the student does not respond correctly to this question, the teacher moves down a step to simple imitation (step 4)—"Say *log*. Good. *Log* rhymes with *frog*." When the teacher reaches a point where the student responds correctly, she then moves back up the staircase, stopping at each step, until the student is able to provide a correct response to the original task. In this example, if the student responds correctly after step 3, then the teacher repeats step 2 by saying, "Does *log* rhyme with *frog*?" After the student provides a correct response to step 2, the teacher then praises and repeats step 1, the original task, "What is a word that rhymes with *frog*?"

For struggling readers, the staircase correction procedure is ideal for several reasons. First, if a student does not produce the correct answer, the teacher provides a prompt at the next step, which reduces the cognitive demand placed on the student. This scaffold creates less effort on the student's part when asked to produce the response to the original task. For example, if the student correctly responds to step 3 and says "*log,*" then when the student is asked to respond to "What is a word that rhymes with *frog*?" he or she is likely to respond "*log.*" Second, since students who need intervention are not often praised (because they do not respond or respond incorrectly) during whole group situations, the staircase approach allows students to be praised more often. The teacher provides easier tasks until the student is correct and then goes back up the staircase, praising with each correct response. At times this may mean a student is praised three or four times through the various steps in the staircase. Traditionally, when a student is incorrect, teachers either choose another student to produce the correct answer, tell the student to choose someone to give the correct answer, or the teacher gives the answer. Using the staircase approach allows the teacher to provide prompts and praise in order to support the student reaching the correct answer. Third, teachers do not need to move directly from the original task to providing the answer. There are several steps in between that allow the teacher to provide only the number of prompts and level of prompting necessary to get the correct answer. Finally, if the teacher takes the student down the staircase, the teacher has to go back up the staircase. This creates a situation in which the student is required to respond to the original prompt. Therefore, the student meets the objective of the lesson.

There needs to be at least four steps in the staircase, and there may be more, depending on the target skill. These four steps include:

- Step 1: Provide a question or task related to the objective.

- Step 2: Binary choice. Offer a yes/no option for the student.

- Step 3: Imitation/modeling. Provide a model for the correct response and then immediately ask the original prompt.

- Step 4: Simple imitation. Tell the student the answer and have them repeat it.

These four steps are shown in the example in Figure 6.3. As the task becomes more difficult, additional steps can be added to ensure that you are using the least number of prompts and level of prompting necessary. (See the blending and the decoding examples in Box 6.3, which includes interactions between teacher and student using the staircase approach.)

The staircase approach is the hallmark principle of the Core Intervention Model and is based on sound research and educational theory. Several studies have demonstrated that the staircase approach to correction procedures is effective for struggling readers (Filippini, 2008; Gerber et al., 2004; Leafstedt et al., 2004; Richards et al., 2006; Solari & Gerber, 2008). Across these studies, the staircase approach has been used by teachers, graduate researchers, and even undergraduate tutors. In these studies, most struggling readers achieved growth and caught up with peers in early reading skills. Why does the staircase approach work? The staircase approach reflects a synthesis of several learning theories but relies most heavily on information-processing and behavioral theories. Information-processing theory explains that every human being has a limited amount of "space," or capacity, to process information (Baddeley, 1986). If a teacher requires a student to perform a task that is effortful—that is, there is either too much information to process or it requires an elaborate response—the student may not have the capacity to perform the task. In this case, the teacher can reduce the demand placed on the student by simplifying the task so that it requires less effort and becomes automatic.

Box 6.3

Teacher-Student Interactions Illustrating the Staircase Approach to Providing Corrective Feedback

Lesson Objective: Students will blend four- to five-phoneme words.

Ms. Perry: Yvonne, what word am I saying? /S/-/t/-/a/-/ck/. (*step 1*)

Yvonne: *Sack.*

Ms. Perry: What word am I saying? /St/-/a/-/ck/. (*step 2: break up the word into fewer phonemes*)

Yvonne: *Stack.*

Ms. Perry: Great job. What word am I saying? /S/-/t/-/a/-/ck/. (*Returning up the staircase*)

Yvonne: *Stack.*

Ms. Perry: Excellent, let's try another one. What word am I saying? /B/-/r/-/ea/-/k/.

[If the student does not give the correct response after step 2, step 3 is to break it down into only onset and rime (/st/-/ack/), step 4 is to give a binary choice (yes/no) question ("Did I say *stack*?"), and step 5 is to tell the answer ("I said *stack*.") and then have the student repeat the word ("*Stack*. Say *stack*.").]

Lesson Objective: Student will read connected text with words that contain consonant blends.

Mr. Lee: Read this sentence. (*Points to the text that reads,* "The boys ran fast.")

Daniel: The boys ran f-a-, I don't know.

Mr. Lee: Point to the word that begins with *f*. Read the word. (*step 1*)

Daniel: F-a-s.

Mr. Lee: What sounds do these letters make? (*Points to* st*; step 3*)

Daniel: /st/

Mr. Lee: Great. Point to the word that begins with *f*. Read the word. (*Returning up the staircase; step 2*)

Daniel: /f/-/a/-/s/-/t/, fast.

Mr. Lee: That is awesome! Read this sentence. (*Returning up the staircase; step 3*)

Daniel: The boys ran fast.

[If the student does not give the correct response at step 3, the teacher goes to step 4, which is a yes/no choice—"Is the word *fast*?"; step 5 is "The word is *fast*. Read it."; and step 6 is "*Fast*. The word is *fast*. Say it."]

The staircase approach starts with a task demand based on the objective; then, if the student poses an incorrect response or no response, the teacher simplifies the original demand and provides another opportunity for response. If the student is still not able to respond, a scaffold, or prompt, is provided until the student can respond. From a cognitive perspective, the levels of prompts reduce the cognitive demand placed on the student and allow a response that requires less effort. Essentially, each step down the staircase is a simplification of the previous step and a scaffold for the student (Vygotsky, 1962). The simplification of the steps of the staircase should follow a **system of least prompts,** which is derived from behavioral theory. This means that the teacher only provides the number of prompts and level of prompting necessary for the student to achieve the correct response (Wolery & Gast, 1984).

Just as the CIM is based heavily on the principles of direct instruction, the staircase correction procedures are grounded in direct instruction approaches to correction (Engelmann & Carnine, 1982). Similar to the CIM, direct instruction models rely on the teacher to control the pace, minimize student error, and have correction procedures at the ready. Direct instruction correction procedures involve the three-step method: model, lead, and test. If a student makes an error, the teacher models the correct answer; then leads the student to the correct answer by saying, "Do it with me"; and finally tests the student to do it independently. The staircase approach enhances this method by providing several levels of prompting to meet the individual needs of students. The "steps" in the staircase provide students the opportunity to be given prompts that they can then generalize to the next task, or demand, placed on them. For example, Box 6.3 shows the interaction between Mr. Lee and Daniel as Mr. Lee uses the staircase approach to provide corrective feedback to Daniel in decoding the word *fast*, a CVCC word. In the staircase, Mr. Lee provides Daniel a prompt to help him blend the consonants *s* and *t*. By using the staircase correction procedures, Mr. Lee has helped Daniel generalize this skill to the next word he reads. When Daniel reads the next word, *nest*, he reads it correctly.

As teachers begin to use the correction staircase, common questions arise. These are explored in Box 6.4.

Box 6.4.

Questions about Using the Staircase Approach

1. *Do I need to use the staircase each time a student makes an error?* During intervention, you want to use the staircase to lead students to the correct response each time they make an error on the target skill, which is essentially your objective.

2. *I have a student with whom I went all the way down and back up the staircase, and he was still not able to get to the correct response. What should I do?* In this case, it is likely that the task is too difficult for the student. Therefore, you should change the objective for the student to reflect his skill level. If, for example, the original objective was to segment three-phoneme words, the new objective should be to break down the word into onset and rime.

3. *Every time one student has an opportunity to respond, I need to use the staircase with him. What should I do?* If you have a student who is consistently making errors with the same task, then, the task is likely too difficult and you will need to change the objective for that student.

4. *If I am focusing on one student using the staircase, what should the other students be doing?* Once you become fluent in using the staircase, it should only take a few seconds to go through the steps with an individual student. However, this can become a concern in the case of more complex tasks in which the staircase is "taller." One way to address this is to have students pair with each other. For example, if you are having students spell words, have students read the words they just spelled to each other. Another idea is to quickly give the other students a new word to spell and, as they are working, focus on the individual student who needs the corrective feedback.

5. *It is sometimes difficult during intervention to think about what my next level of the staircase should be. What should I do?* It is best to have at least one staircase template for each objective you have in an intervention lesson. Preparing this template ahead of time will give you a guide to use if a student makes an error. Chapter 8 provides several examples.

Conducting Interventions
Using the Six Principles

109

Chapter Six
How Should I
Teach It?

Remembering to use each of the six principles of the CIM is difficult, especially when first conducting interventions. In our research using the Early Reading Project Intervention, teachers used a checklist of teaching procedures that incorporated the six principles of the CIM (Leafstedt et al., 2004; Richards et al., 2006). When conducting interventions, it is useful to have this checklist at hand, along with a short lesson plan that includes a sample of the staircase. The nine components in the checklist fit within the six principles described in detail above. (See Table 6.3.) The checklist for the early Reading Project Intervention is included in Chapter 8, Appendix 8.8.

TABLE 6.3 Components of Intervention and Corresponding CIM Principles

Checklist Component	CIM Principle
Three to four students in a group	Small groups
State objectives	Specific objectives
Model activity	Explicit and intensive teaching of skills
Break down activities into steps	Content and materials are appropriate
Guided practice	Explicit and intensive teaching of skills
Praise students often for correct responses	Corrective feedback
Provide many opportunities for students to respond	Opportunities for many correct responses
Use the staircase	Corrective feedback
Teach skills to mastery	Explicit and intensive teaching of skills

Summary

The Core Intervention Model has six principles that allow teachers to **differentiate** intervention for individual students:

1. Conduct intervention in small groups of ideally three to four students.

2. Write observable and measurable objectives for each lesson.

3. Choose appropriate content and materials for each lesson and for each individual student, based on screening and progress-monitoring assessments.

4. Teach skills explicitly, intensively, and at a rapid pace. This includes modeling each activity and providing opportunities for guided practice and independent practice.

5. Maximize the number of student responses during intervention lessons.

6. Use the staircase approach to provide corrective feedback to students.

The Data-Based Decision-Making Cycle

Objectives

By the end of this chapter, the reader will be able to

1. Define data-based decision making

2. Articulate the three phases of data-based decision making for early reading interventions

3. Describe the stages of data-based decision making at each of the three phases

This chapter is designed to provide a detailed description of the organization of intervention from beginning (i.e., selecting students for intervention) to end (i.e., exiting students from intervention). Whereas Chapters 5 and 6 covered the content and methods for early reading intervention, Chapter 7 provides the nuts and bolts for determining who needs intervention; if intervention is effective; and how and when to start, modify, or end intervention. These processes are presented through the data-based decision-making cycle.

Data-Based Decision Making

Data-based decision making (DBDM) is a cyclical process in which data are used to make instructional and curricular decisions. Data-based decision making can be used for classroom, schoolwide, and districtwide decisions. The DBDM cycle involves four stages: data collection, analysis and reflection, instructional planning, and providing instruction (see Figure 7.1). Essentially, DBDM is the process of collecting and using data to guide instruction. For purposes of classroom or grade level-intervention, DBDM can be thought of in three phases—before, during, and after an **intervention session**, which is typically a 10-week period. In each phase of the cycle, the stages are generally the same, but there are specific differences that warrant each phase being discussed separately. (See Figure 7.2.)

FIGURE 7.1   **The Data-Based Decision-Making Cycle**

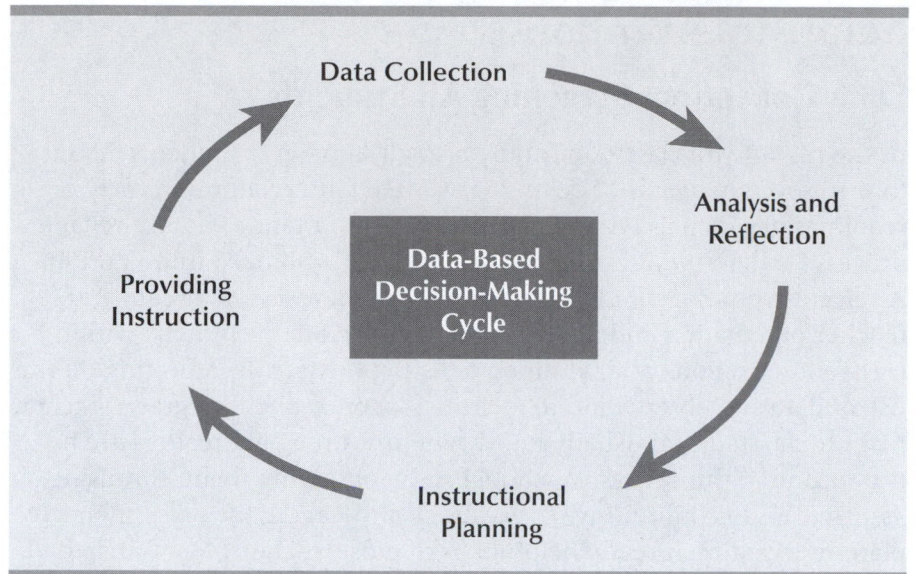

FIGURE 7.2   **Data-Based Decision Making**
before Intervention

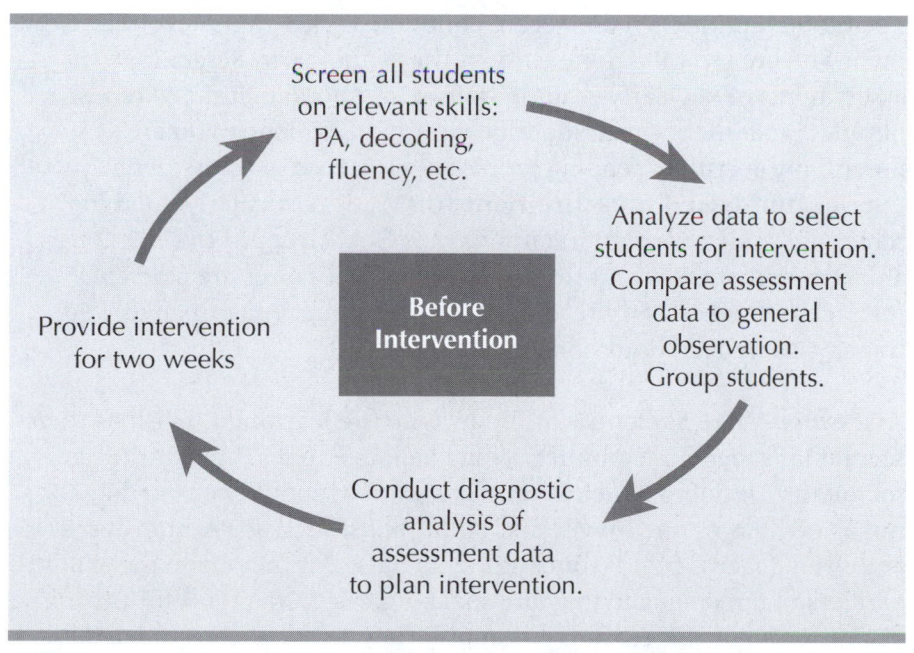

Data-Based Decision Making before Intervention

Data Collection: Screening All Students

In the majority of classrooms, only a small number of students, about four to seven in a class of 20 or 25, will need intervention in early reading skills such as PA and phonics. It is important to have a reliable process for determining who the students are who need intervention. A selection process should incorporate student assessment data and teacher observation and allow for the comparison of students within a classroom, a school, and, at times, a district or state. In reflecting on the use of data and observation to identify students, one first-grade teacher, Ms. Garcia, stated, "I usually know who my struggling readers are by the second or third week of school just by observing them. But using assessments to confirm my observations and having the assessments to plan intervention is really helpful." Like most teachers, Ms. Garcia had a good sense of who the struggling students were in her class but wanted a way to validate her observations with assessments. She then used the assessment data to determine what her students already knew and what they still needed to be taught.

Screening assessments are used to determine which students need intervention. Screenings are conducted with grade-level assessment and are typically done early in the school year. Screening assessments of key early reading skills (i.e., phonological awareness, phonics, and fluency) can identify a group of students who are potentially at risk for reading problems. One type of assessment, **curriculum-based measurement** (CBM), is particularly good for screening students for intervention. (See Box 7.1, pp. 116–117, for a description of CBM and resources.) These measures are available for each of the key early reading skills: PA, alphabetic principle, and fluency, as well as comprehension.

Assessment of EL Students.   Students who are learning English as their second language pose an interesting challenge to teachers during assessments. Deciding which language a student should be tested in is not as obvious as one may think. Some skills, such as PA, transfer across languages. That is, once students have PA, they have the skill regardless of the language they are speaking. (See Chapter 3 for further discussion.) For this reason, it is appropriate to assess the students in their first language on PA measures, even if it is not the language of instruction. Assessing students in their first language may be especially important for students coming to school for the first time (generally in kindergarten or first grade) or students coming to school in the United States for the first time who are not familiar with English. It is often the case that a student who is new to the country appears behind in many skills because of the time it takes to acquire English. When testing students in their native language, teachers can better pinpoint which skills students have already acquired in their native language and will apply to English reading when their English has sufficiently developed. Although some reading skills transfer across languages, not all skills do. Alphabetic principle, for instance, needs to be assessed and taught in the language of instruction because letters and sounds are unique to the specific language. If students have strong alphabetic principle in their native language, this will assist them in reading in English. However, since English has different letters and sounds and different rules for these relationships, phonics will need to be taught in English.

For ELs, it is recommended that initial screenings in early reading skills be conducted in both the language of instruction and the student's primary language. If students perform well in their primary language, even if they do not perform well in English, they will likely make gains in these skills in a short time in English as they develop English language proficiency. If students perform below expectations in both languages, they should be provided with intervention for early reading skills in addition to English language development. In some instances, it is not an option to assess the student in her or his primary language, because assessments are not available or the educators at the school site do not speak the student's primary language. If there is an educator at the site that does speak the student's primary language, using an assessment that allows the teacher to provide directions in the student's primary language will ensure that the student understands the task. However, if the teacher or another educator does not speak the student's primary language, then it is essential to make sure that the student understands the task of the assessments. In this case, choosing an assessment that has practice items and using visual cues will be useful.

Assessment of Students with Learning Disabilities. The vast majority of students in K through 3 who are identified to receive special education services for a learning disability will need reading intervention. Therefore, it is not necessary to screen these students to determine if they need intervention. However, initial grade-level assessments do need

Box 7.1

Collecting the Data to Make Decisions— Curriculum-Based Measurement

Curriculum-based measurement (CBM) is a reliable and valid method for determining who needs intervention as well as for monitoring student growth in reading skills. CBM is the most widely available and most well researched tool available for collecting ongoing data during intervention (Wallace et al., 2007). CBM was designed specifically to monitor student progress. CBM provides data to determine the efficacy of the intervention (i.e., students are making progress) and also the instructional needs of individual students (Deno, 1985). The measures were created to be reliable and valid and also to be practical so that teachers could administer the assessments quickly and interpret the scores of the assessments easily (Deno, 1985). Many CBM assessments have multiple forms of the same measure in order to administer screening and progress-monitoring assessments multiple times.

The skills measured using CBM need to be indicators of overall reading performance. In the area of reading, CBM assessment of skills includes letter knowledge, phonological awareness, word reading, and nonsense word reading as well as passage reading and comprehension. Although districts and schools have assessments that measure these skills, they are often mastery assessments. Mastery assessments are not effective for frequent progress monitoring, for two reasons. First, many mastery assessments are not valid and reliable. Second, because mastery assessments only give students credit if they have mastered the skill, they do not show changes in short periods of time. On the other hand, because CBM measures students' initial performance and shows progress on a skill, small changes in student growth are seen even if the student has not mastered the skill (Fuchs, Fuchs & Hamlett, 1993). Additionally, CBM taps into how fluent, or quick and accurate, a student is with the skill.

For ELs, some studies have been conducted that indicate that CBM of early reading skills can be a powerful tool for identifying students in need of intervention and for monitoring student progress (Wayman, Wallace & Wiley, 2007). However, there is some research that indicates that oral reading fluency, a common CBM, may underidentify students who are EL for intervention. Some ELs will master decoding skills and be able to read fluently but, due to a limited English vocabulary and weak comprehension skills, may not understand what they read. Therefore, if ELs read a passage fluently, it is important to check for understanding. For students who are already identified as having learning disabilities, these measures are also reliable and valid. CBM was originally designed for students in special education, and much of the research on CBM includes students with disabilities (Wayman et al., 2007).

CBM Resources

AIMSWeb

http://aimsweb.com/

AIMSWeb is a Web-based system that provides progress-monitoring assessments, all curriculum-based measures, storage of data, and programs to analyze and report the data. AIMSWeb costs $3 to $5 per student, depending on the package.

CBM Warehouse

www.interventioncentral.org/htmdocs/interventions/cbmwarehouse.php

Intervention Central offers CBM Warehouse, which has many early reading and reading fluency assessments available as well as free programs to create your own assessments. All measures are free to download on the Website or by contacting authors of the assessments. Spanish measures are also available for some assessments.

Dynamic Indicators of Basic Early Literacy Skills (DIBELS)

http://dibels.uoregon.edu/

DIBELS includes assessments for kindergarten through sixth grade. On the Website, the assessments for each grade level are provided as well as the benchmark scores for each grade and assessment. The measures are also available in Spanish (Indicadores Dinámicos del Éxito en la Lectura-IDEL) for kindergarten through third grade. All measures are available for free on the Website. DIBELS also offers a data management system for entering, storing, analyzing, and reporting assessment data, from $1 per student.

National Center on Student Progress Monitoring

www.studentprogress.org

The National Center on Student Progress Monitoring provides resources for educators and families regarding progress monitoring. Under the TOOLS section, there is a list of many progress-monitoring measures and whether they have met specified standards. The center also offers free Web seminars about progress monitoring related to both general and special education.

to be administered to determine target skills for intervention and to help form intervention groups. The initial assessment also provides a baseline score so that student growth can be monitored.

Analysis and Reflection: Selecting Students for Intervention

Once all students in a class or grade level have been screened using grade-level assessments, students in need of intervention can be selected. Making a table of student scores is usually the simplest way to analyze the assessment data. (See Table 7.1, p. 120, for an example.) To select students for intervention, both assessment data and general classroom observations should be used for analysis and reflection. At times, there can be a discrepancy between assessment data and observation. In this case, it is best to reconcile the discrepancy by conducting additional screening assessment with the student. For example, if a student's screening assessment indicates need for intervention on beginning fluency yet the teacher has seen the student read fluently, a second fluency assessment should be given. At this point, if student performance is still below expectations, the student should be included in the intervention and progress should be monitored.

At times, screening measures can overidentify students in need of intervention, particularly in kindergarten and first grade (Fuchs & Fuchs, 2007; Speece & Walker, 2007). Therefore, teacher observation and judgment play a key role. Research suggests that teachers should complement their screenings by monitoring the progress of their students using CBM for five weeks (Fuchs & Fuchs, 2007). Students who make adequate progress during the five weeks are generally doing well with general classroom instruction and are not in need of intervention even if they perform poorly on the screening. Students who do not make progress toward their goal on curriculum-based measures with only general instruction should receive intervention.

Approximately 20 to 30 percent of students in a given classroom, grade level, or school will be in need of intervention (Vaughn & Roberts, 2007; Vaughn et al., 2007), which is about 4 to 10 students in a single class, depending on the class size. If a teacher finds that over 30 percent of the students in the class are in need of intervention, then it is a good idea to reflect on how to modify general classroom reading instruction to meet the needs of the students in the class. Adding more activities that focus on early reading skills to the general curriculum may help many students.

After students have been identified for intervention based on analysis and reflection on data, they should be grouped according to need. Grouping should be based on careful analysis of screening assessment data. All student data should be examined to look for students who performed similarly. For example in a first-grade class, one intervention group may focus primarily on PA while another may focus on phonics, teaching the alphabetic principle.

Table 7.1 shows the screening data from Ms. Perry's first-grade class at the beginning of the year. The data show that there are individual differences among students who struggle with reading. Examining data on each student allows for a more careful look at the individual students and their skills. Individual data allow Ms. Perry to group students according to need and to design intervention to meet individual student needs. The scores in Table 7.1 are from two measures—segmentation fluency (a PA assessment) and nonsense word fluency (an assessment of alphabetic principle)—from Dynamic Indicators of Basic Early Literacy Skills (DIBELS) (Good & Kaminski, 2002). These are one-minute timed assessments, and the scores indicate sounds per minute. Segmentation fluency measures PA by asking the students to say the individual sounds they hear in words with two to five phonemes. Nonsense word fluency measures alphabetic principle by having students either tell the letter sounds from three-phoneme nonwords or read the nonwords. As the data indicate, there are several students who struggled with both PA and alphabetic principle at the beginning of the year and others who only struggled with the alphabetic principle. (Using the DIBELS benchmarks, students considered at risk or at some risk are noted in Table 7.1.)

Looking at the data from Ms. Perry's class, seven students have needs in early reading skills, four have needs in PA and alphabetic principle, and three only have needs in alphabetic principle. Students who have deficits in the same areas should be grouped together to the greatest extent possible. Ideally, Ms. Perry will create two groups for intervention, because the needs of the students differ. Also, in this case a group of seven would be too large to meet individual needs. (Recall that principle 1 of the CIM is small groups, ideally three to four students.) Since language development is not part of the intervention, ELs should be grouped according to early reading ability, not language ability. Grouping heterogeneously by language level can benefit those students who have the lowest language levels. For Ms. Perry's class, the two intervention groups are shown in Table 7.2

TABLE 7.1 Record of Initial English Language Levels and DIBELS Scores for Ms. Perry's Class

Student Name	English Language Level	Segmentation Fluency (goal = 35)	Nonsense Word Fluency (goal = 24)
Candice	Advanced	36	40
Michael	Proficient	35	42
Jacob	EO	38	45
Yvonne[a]	Intermediate	15	8
Monica[b]	Advanced	36	14
Lee	Intermediate	35	24
Ben[a]	EO	9	1
Alex	Beginning	40	26
Tyler	EO	45	47
Leslie[b]	Beginning	37	18
Vanessa	EO	40	28
Isabel	Advanced	37	26
Humberto[a]	Proficient	16	15
Marissa	EO	43	30
Brenda[a]	Advanced	14	19
Arianna	Intermediate	47	29
Kevin[b]	EO	39	19
Vivian	Proficient	35	24
Francesca	Proficient	41	24
Mario	Advanced	50	31
Kyle	EO	38	27
Ryana	EO	40	33
Juliana	Advanced	42	40

[a]Student is below benchmark in both PA and alphabetic principle.
[b]Student is below benchmark only in alphabetic principle.
Note: EO = English only.

TABLE 7.2 **Ms. Perry's Two Intervention Groups**

Group 1	Group 2
Yvonne	Monica
Ben	Leslie
Humberto	Kevin
Brenda	

For students already identified with LD, the screening data will assist general and special educators in determining how to group students across grades or how to fit a student with LD into a group already established in the general education classroom. For example, Mr. Lee, the special educator, has a first-grade student, Ryan, on his caseload, who was not in need of intervention in PA (scoring at benchmark on segmentation fluency) but was in need of intervention in alphabetic principle (scoring an 18 on nonsense word fluency). This student would fit perfectly in Ms. Perry's group 2. By participating in intervention in Ms. Perry's class, Ryan will receive extra intervention to meet his needs while complementing Ms. Perry's classroom structure.

Mr. Lee also has a third-grade student, Daniel, on his caseload, whom he tried to fit into a group in either Daniel's third-grade class or another third-grade class. However, Daniel scored a 10 on the third-grade DIBELS reading fluency measure that Mr. Lee administered. There was not an existing intervention group of third-grade students in Daniel's class who had the same needs as Daniel. Mr. Lee decided to put Daniel with another third-grader and two other fourth-grade students from other classes with similar needs and work with them in the school's learning center.

Instructional Planning—Setting Goals and Designing Intervention

After students have been selected for intervention, it is time to plan. The first step in planning is to decide what the overall **goals** for intervention will be for each student and each group. This process involves looking deeper into the assessment data to "diagnose" what areas the students need to focus on within the scope and sequence of the Early Reading Project Intervention. Screening measures can provide teachers with detailed information about where to begin instruction and what the strengths and needs of the students are related to early reading skills. For example, Figure 7.3 shows Yvonne's performance on the PA assessment and the alphabetic principle assessment. Looking at Yvonne's assessment data, specific patterns can be found that can guide intervention. On the PA assessment, on which Yvonne needs to segment words presented orally, the data show that she has a pattern of not hearing the medial vowel; in some cases, she also misses initial blends and ending sounds. Her strengths are initial sounds. On the alphabetic principle assessment, Yvonne demonstrates a need to increase her knowledge of letter sounds, especially vowel sounds. It is unclear which consonant sounds she knows, and further assessment of all letter sounds would provide more information to Ms. Perry. These data also show that Yvonne is not yet blending sounds together to read words.

After looking at a sample of Yvonne's data, Ms. Perry feels that Yvonne's screening measures do not provide enough information to develop intervention and that additional testing is necessary. If the screening measures are not sufficient for setting goals for intervention, the

FIGURE 7.3   PA and Alphabetic Principle Task Data Sheet for Yvonne

Segmentation task. Words are said aloud to Yvonne. She is then asked to repeat the sounds in words.

CAT   LOG   FROG   BET   BUN   DAD   LINT

Alphabetic principle task. Yvonne reads the letter sounds aloud or reads the words.

buf   din   gom   sut   lef   pak

Note: Examples modeled after DIBELS phoneme segmentation fluency and nonsense word fluency assessments.

teacher should consider administering additional assessments. Ms. Perry decides to give Yvonne a letter-sound knowledge assessment. Common assessments for gathering more information include letter-sound knowledge assessments, PA assessments in rhyming and/or blending, and phonics or decoding assessments. When choosing additional assessments, a teacher should choose a tool that provides detailed information about a student's mastery of a skill (i.e., exact letter sounds they can identify, number of phonemes they can blend orally, letter combinations they can read, specific text reading level that matches to leveled readers, etc.). Many school sites have assessments that will provide this more detailed diagnostic information, such as the Developmental Reading Inventory (DRA), the CORE Phonics Survey, or the Basic Phonics Skills Test. Having several sources of data will assist in determining the target skill for intervention and the goal for intervention. After conducting further assessment on the exact letter sounds Yvonne can identify, Ms. Perry determines that Yvonne has most consonant sounds except for *n, d,* and *w,* all of which she confuses with sounds of other letters (i.e., she says /m/ for *n,* /b/ for *d,* and /u/ for *w*); also, she does not know any of the vowel sounds except *a.* Based on all of these data, Ms. Perry set the following goal for intervention for Yvonne: By the end of the 10-week intervention, Yvonne will segment and blend three- and four-phoneme words; will identify all letter sounds in a word; and will manipulate the beginning, middle, and final phonemes in a word using letter tiles (i.e., changing *cat* to *mat*).

For students, especially those with LD, it may be difficult to plan for intervention based on analysis of a student's initial screening measure because the student is performing significantly below grade level and therefore cannot perform enough of the task to provide any informative data. In these cases, further assessment is needed to identify the student's instructional level. To do this, the teacher tests down a grade level until the student's **instructional reading level** is determined. For example, Mr. Lee assessed Daniel, and Daniel scored a 10 on the third-grade oral reading fluency screen from the DIBELS assessments. Mr. Lee then gave Daniel the second-grade fluency screen. Daniel did better, but still only scored a 20 and only read 35 words (15 errors), remaining well below benchmark. Mr. Lee then gave Daniel the first-grade screen in which he scored a 48 and read 50 words (two errors). Mr. Lee determined that first-grade passages are Daniel's instructional level. Mr. Lee then planned intervention based on Daniel's instructional level and the error analysis from the passages he read.

Let's return to Ms. Perry's class and look at the group of students chosen for intervention in Yvonne's group. Based on the data from Yvonne and the other students in her group selected for intervention, an intervention plan for the first two weeks can be outlined. Ms. Percy set the following overall goal for intervention for Yvonne and the other students:

> By the end of the 10-week intervention, students in group 1 will segment and blend three- and four-phoneme words; will identify all letter sounds in a word; and will manipulate the beginning, middle, and final phonemes in a word using letter tiles (i.e., changing *cat* to *mat*).

Ms. Perry sets two objectives for the first two weeks of intervention that are steps to reaching this goal. Ms. Perry uses the two-week intervention plan (see Table 7.3) to guide her intervention lessons. She then uses the intervention lesson plan for daily lessons to detail the lesson's activities. (See the lesson sample in Figure 6.2, p. 99.) Ms. Perry will provide students in Yvonne's group 20 minutes of intervention four days each week.

When planning for intervention for his students identified with LD, Mr. Lee considers the data from the assessments but also considers the student's IEP goals. Daniel has a reading fluency IEP goal that states, "By June 15, after receiving direct instruction in small group, Daniel will read a second-grade passage at 80 words per minute as measured by a DIBELS second-grade reading passage." Based on the data, and in line with Daniel's IEP goal, Mr. Lee set the following goals for intervention:

> At the end of 10 weeks, Daniel will decode short vowel words with consonant blends (i.e., CVCC, CCVC, CCVCC) and long vowel words with silent *e* (CVCe), and he will increase his reading fluency on first-grade passages.

The two-week intervention plan Mr. Lee developed for Daniel and the other students in the group is displayed in Table 7.4. Mr. Lee provides these students intervention for 45 minutes, four days a week. He spends 35 minutes on PA, phonics, and fluency skills and then changes to vocabulary development and comprehension strategies for 10 minutes. Because these students are older and need more intensive intervention to meet grade-level standards in reading, Mr. Lee must attend to their vocabulary and comprehension as well.

TABLE 7.3 Two-Week Intervention Plan for Ms. Perry's Group 1

Objective 1: Students will be able to segment and blend three-phoneme words orally using -it, -ad, and -ed word families.

Objective 2: Students will be able to identify all vowel sounds when presented with the written letters.

Day	Phonics (5 min.)	PA (7 min.)	PA (8 min.)	Notes
Monday *Target skill:* Blending 3-phoneme words; segmenting 3-phoneme words; manipulating beginning sound in words; word families: -it, -ad, -en	Flashcards. Review letter sounds, including all vowels.	Guess-My-Word game. Grab bag with 3- and 4-phoneme words. Choose a picture out of the bag; say the name of picture segmented (e.g., /b/-/a/-/t/).	Segmenting. Tapping sounds (bit, hit, mit, pit, kit, rad, mad, sad, lad, bad, den, ten, men, pen).	
Tuesday/Wednesday *Target skill:* Same ⟶				
Friday *Target skill:* Blending 3-phoneme words; segmenting 3-phoneme words; manipulating beginning sound in words	Flashcards. Review letter sounds, including vowels.	Grab bag. Blending 4-phoneme words. Segmenting. Tapping sounds.	Spelling CVC words, given the rime portion of the word (-at; spell *cat*), and reading the CVC words.	
Monday/Tuesday *Target skill:* Same ⟶				
Wednesday/Thursday *Target skill:* Same	Flashcards. Review letter sounds, including vowels.	Grab bag. Blending 4-phoneme words. Manipulating initial sound in words.	Spelling CVC words, given the rime portion of the word (-at; spell *cat*), and reading the CVC words.	
Friday ASSESS!!!!	Notes for next sessions:			

TABLE 7.4 Two-Week Intervention Plan for Mr. Lee's Group, Including Daniel

Objective 1: Students will be able to decode short vowel words CCVC (bl-, pl-, cl-, sl-).

Objective 2: Students will be able to decode CCVC words in connected text.

Day	PA (5 min.)	Phonics (20 min.)	Fluency (10 min.)	Notes
Monday *Target skill:* Decoding short vowel words CVCC	Review segmenting words with 4 phonemes.	Introduce bl- and cl-. Spelling CVCC words and manipulating beginning and ending sounds in words to make new words to read	Read passage with CVCC words.	
Tuesday/Wednesday *Target skill:* Same	Review segmenting words with 4 phonemes.	Review bl-, cl-. Spelling CVCC words and manipulating all sounds in words to make new words to read.	Read passage with CVCC words.	
Friday *Target skill:* Decoding words with short vowel CCVC	Review segmenting words with 4 phonemes.	Introduce pl- and sl-. Spelling CVCC words and manipulating beginning and ending sounds in words to make new words to read.	Read passage with CCVC words.	
Monday/Tuesday *Target skill:* Same	Review segmenting words with 4 phonemes.	Review pl- and sl-. Spelling CVCC words and manipulating all sounds in words to make new words to read.	Read passage with CCVC words.	
Wednesday/Thursday *Target skill:* Same	Review segmenting words with 4 phonemes.	Review pl- and sl-. Spelling CVCC words and manipulating all sounds in words to make new words to read	Read passage with CCVC words.	
Friday ASSESS!!!!	Notes for next sessions:			

Instruction: Using the CIM Model

After goals for intervention have been determined and the scope and sequence of the intervention has been planned, intervention is conducted using the methods from the CIM. Recall that the methods used for the CIM are explicit teaching methods, using praise for correct answers, promoting a large number of student responses, and using the staircase correction procedures. During the first two weeks of intervention, teachers should observe student responses closely, noting how each of the students is doing at the end of each lesson to prepare for the next day's intervention lesson. For some groups, teachers will find that they are repeating essentially the same lesson for multiple days. Other groups will catch on very quickly, and new objectives and goals for intervention can be set. Providing instruction using the CIM concludes the before-intervention phase; the cycle now moves to the during-intervention phase.

Data-Based Decision Making during Intervention

Data Collection: Monitoring Student Progress

After the first two weeks of intervention, the DBDM cycle comes full circle and returns to data collection. In the during-intervention phase, data are collected through regular **progress monitoring**. (See Figure 7.4.) Progress monitoring consists of ongoing data collection and is one of the most critical factors of intervention. An intervention, which by definition is targeted to individual student needs, requires ongoing collection of student data to guide and determine the intervention's effectiveness and whether students are making progress toward the goal.

Assessments Used for Progress Monitoring. In order to gain the necessary information for progress monitoring, specific assessments should be selected. CBM (see Box 7.1, pp. 116–117) are ideal for progress monitoring, for several reasons. Curriculum-based measures

- Are quick one-minute assessments that have multiple probes available (multiple forms of the same measures)
- Help guide intervention through error analysis and growth rates
- Motivate students and teachers because they reflect growth

FIGURE 7.4 **Data-Based Decision Making during Intervention**

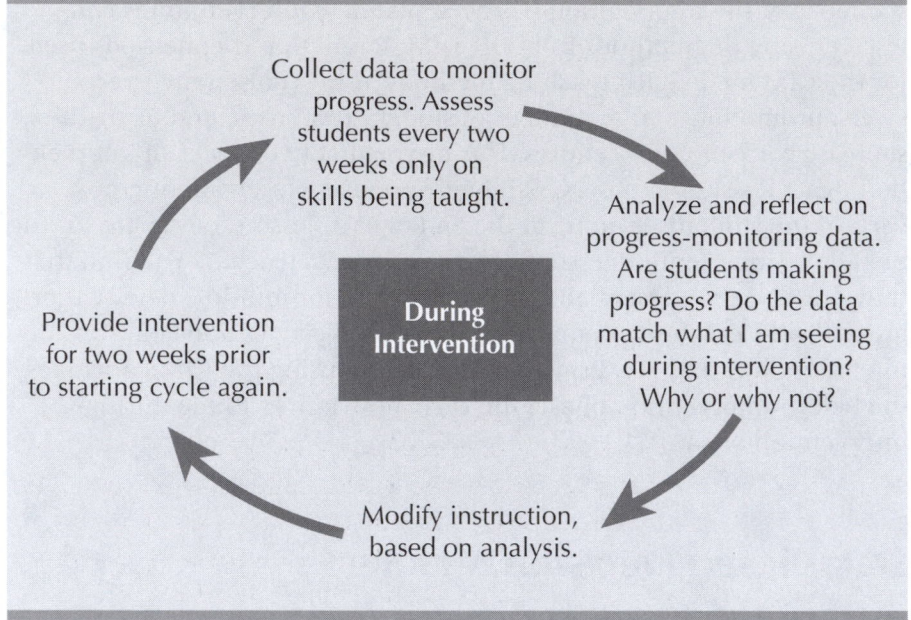

Collect data to monitor progress. Assess students every two weeks only on skills being taught.

Analyze and reflect on progress-monitoring data. Are students making progress? Do the data match what I am seeing during intervention? Why or why not?

During Intervention

Modify instruction, based on analysis.

Provide intervention for two weeks prior to starting cycle again.

- Allow for measuring skill and fluency with the skill through timed assessments
- Can be used for both screening and progress monitoring
- Are appropriate for both ELs and students with LD (For ELs, assess in language of instruction; if assessed in English, provide directions in primary language if assessment allows.)

CBM are available for multiple early reading skills, including PA, alphabetic principle, and reading fluency. Deciding which of these skills to monitor is determined by the goals for intervention. Ongoing progress monitoring should occur for the skills being taught during intervention. Early reading skills closely overlap, and many students will have goals for both PA and phonics skills, with the ultimate goal of attaining reading fluency and comprehension. Therefore, monitoring a combination of the following is recommended: PA, alphabetic principle (to assess phonics), and (as students are ready) the ability to read connected text (which is assessed using fluency measures).

Frequency of Assessment. Ideally, for a student receiving intervention, progress is monitored weekly or biweekly. The lower performing the student, the more often the student should be assessed. By assessing more frequently, modifications to the intervention can be made immediately. If assessments indicate that students are responding well to the intervention, the teacher can continue to progress through the scope and sequence and even accelerate instruction. If the progress-monitoring data indicate a student or students are not responding to the intervention, modifications can be made to further break down skills, review skills, provide more opportunities to respond, extend length of lessons, and so on.

Benchmarks for Measuring Growth. Most curriculum-based measures have benchmarks, or cutoff scores, to determine if students have met the grade-level expectations. These benchmarks are a guide to evaluate student growth over the period of intervention. For example, Yvonne scored 15 on the initial screening of the DIBELS phoneme segmentation fluency measure. The DIBELS benchmark is 35 for segmentation fluency. After 10 weeks of intervention, Ms. Perry wants to see Yvonne reach the benchmark. Generally, on reading measures, the scores obtained are sounds or words correct per minute. Realistic growth rates for early reading skills, PA, alphabetic principle, and reading fluency are typically two sounds or words per week. This holds true for ELs as well (Solari & Richards, 2008). In grades K through 1, students tend to make more growth than students in grades 2 through 3 (Wayman et al., 2007). Therefore, for older students like Daniel, more realistic growth rates on fluency measures are 1 to 1.5 words per week. If Yvonne made a two-sound-per-week growth on phoneme segmentation, she would meet the benchmark at the end of the 10 weeks of intervention.

Analysis and Reflection: Reviewing Progress-Monitoring Data

During intervention, the analysis and reflection stage involves examining progress-monitoring data to see if students are responding to intervention and to determine if instruction needs to be modified. Error analysis of weekly or biweekly progress-monitoring data is particularly useful for making small instructional changes. If a student is doing well in intervention but consistently making errors in decoding words with the /a/ sound in them, this is important to know and address during intervention. Observation during intervention also yields important data for making modifications. Ms. Perry makes comments on her lesson plans to indicate areas where students are doing well or are struggling so she knows what to review and when to move on.

In reflecting on the progress-monitoring and observation data after three weeks of intervention, Ms. Perry was surprised that Humberto was not making more progress on the assessment of alphabetic principle, since he was doing so well during the intervention lessons. Ms. Perry is sure that Humberto is making growth and decides to continue working on the same skills during the lessons but makes certain that Humberto has opportunities for more individual responses and practice. On the next progress-monitoring assessment after four weeks of intervention, she sees that Humberto has made large gains. It is common to have student performance improve during intervention prior to seeing large improvements on the progress-monitoring assessments.

FIGURE 7.5 **Progress-Monitoring Data, Weeks 1 through 5, on Phonological Awareness for Group 1 Students**

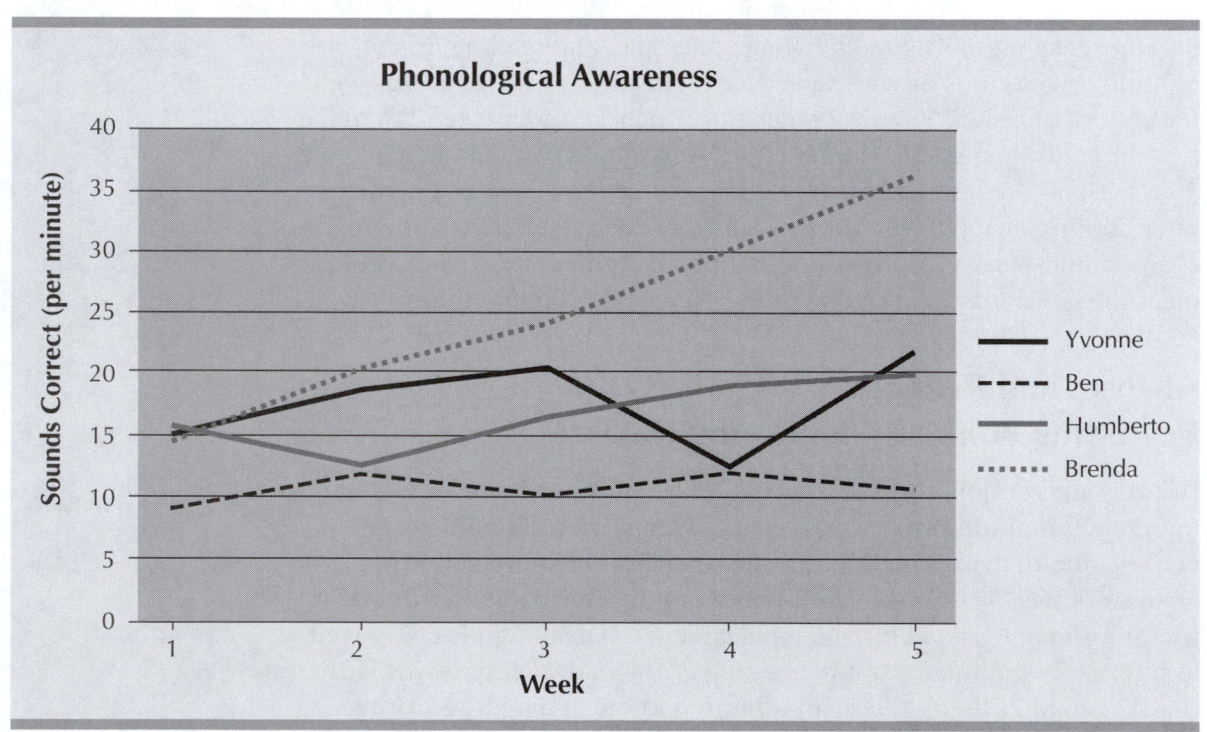

Improvement observed during intervention lessons is a good sign that a student like Humberto is moving toward becoming faster and more accurate with the skills. Often, within another week of intervention, progress is seen on the assessments as well.

After about four to five weeks of intervention, a trend in student data is apparent. At this point, more significant modifications to intervention can be made if necessary. Figures 7.5 and 7.6 show how the first-grade students in group 1 from Ms. Perry's class responded after being provided intervention for five weeks. She collected progress-

FIGURE 7.6 **Progress Monitoring Data on Alphabetic Principle for Students in Group 1**

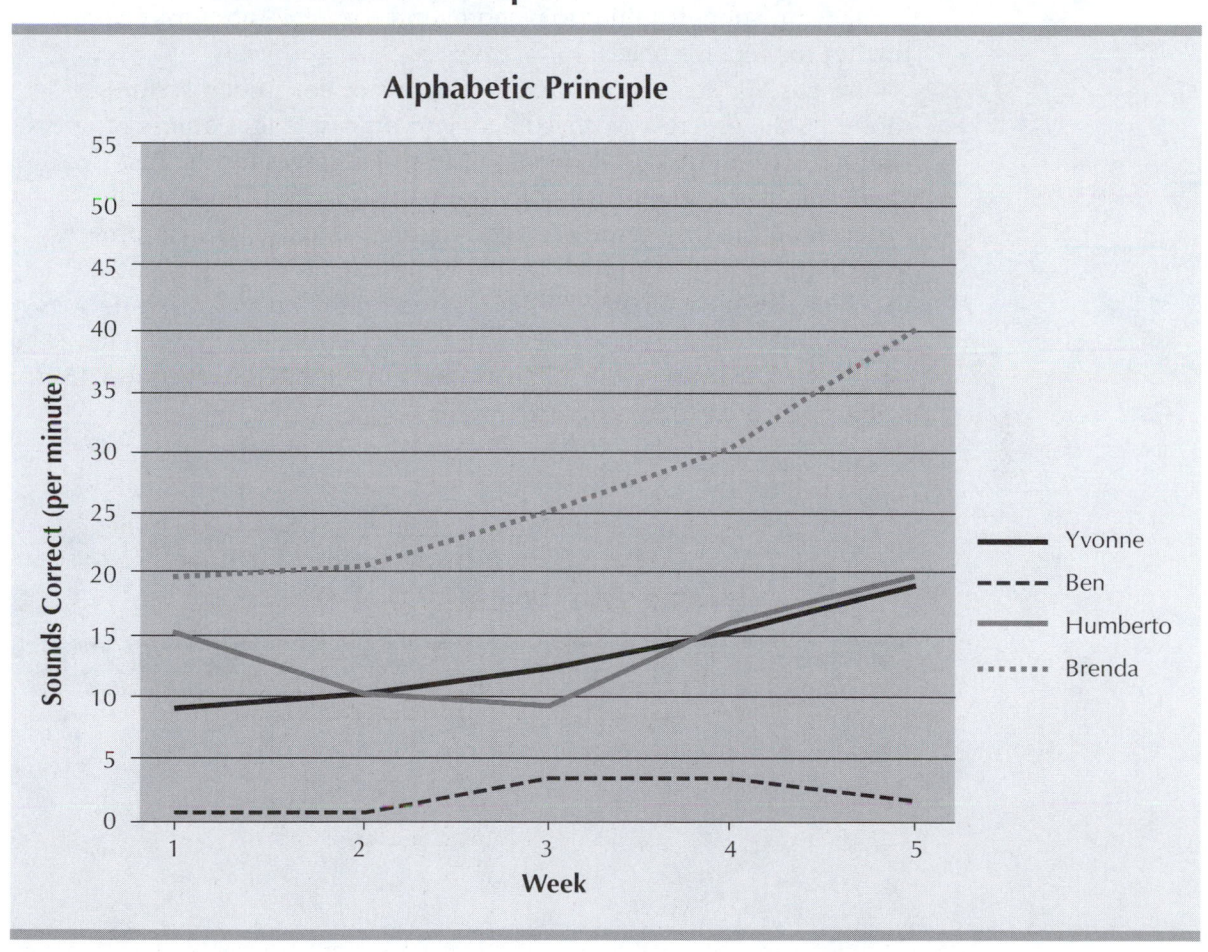

monitoring data each week using DIBELS, so there are five data points to review. When looking at the data, it is clear that Brenda is doing well with the intervention, particularly in PA. Since Brenda has met the PA benchmark, Ms. Perry moves her to group 2, which is working only on phonics skills. Humberto and Yvonne also appear to be responding to the intervention, although slowly. They will need additional intervention in both PA and phonics skills. Ben, on the other hand, is not responding to intervention and is still performing significantly below benchmark and his peers. Modifications to intervention to consider would be more time (up to 30 minutes and/or five days a week) or smaller group size. Ms. Perry decides that group 1 will now receive 30 minutes, five days a week of intervention, and the group will only have three students, since Brenda has moved to group 2. (See Table 7.5.) Ms. Perry also makes instructional adjustments for Ben, making sure that he has more opportunities to respond and that skills are broken down further to meet his needs.

Just as Ms. Perry monitors the progress of her students, Mr. Lee monitors the progress of the students on his caseload. Daniel's progress is monitored on first-grade reading fluency passages for the first five weeks of intervention. During these first five weeks, Daniel made progress on the first-grade passages. Figure 7.7 show Daniel's progress in reading fluency. Although Daniel is making progress, it is not as much as Mr. Lee would like to see. Based on the data, Mr. Lee decides to continue working on phonics and fluency but adds extra fluency practice to the lessons. Mr. Lee continues to provide intervention 45 minutes each day, four days each week.

TABLE 7.5   Ms. Perry's Two Intervention Groups after Five Weeks

Group 1	Group 2
Yvonne	Monica
Ben	Leslie
Humberto	Kevin
	Brenda

FIGURE 7.7 Daniel's Oral Reading Fluency Scores on First-Grade DIBELS Oral Reading Fluency Passages

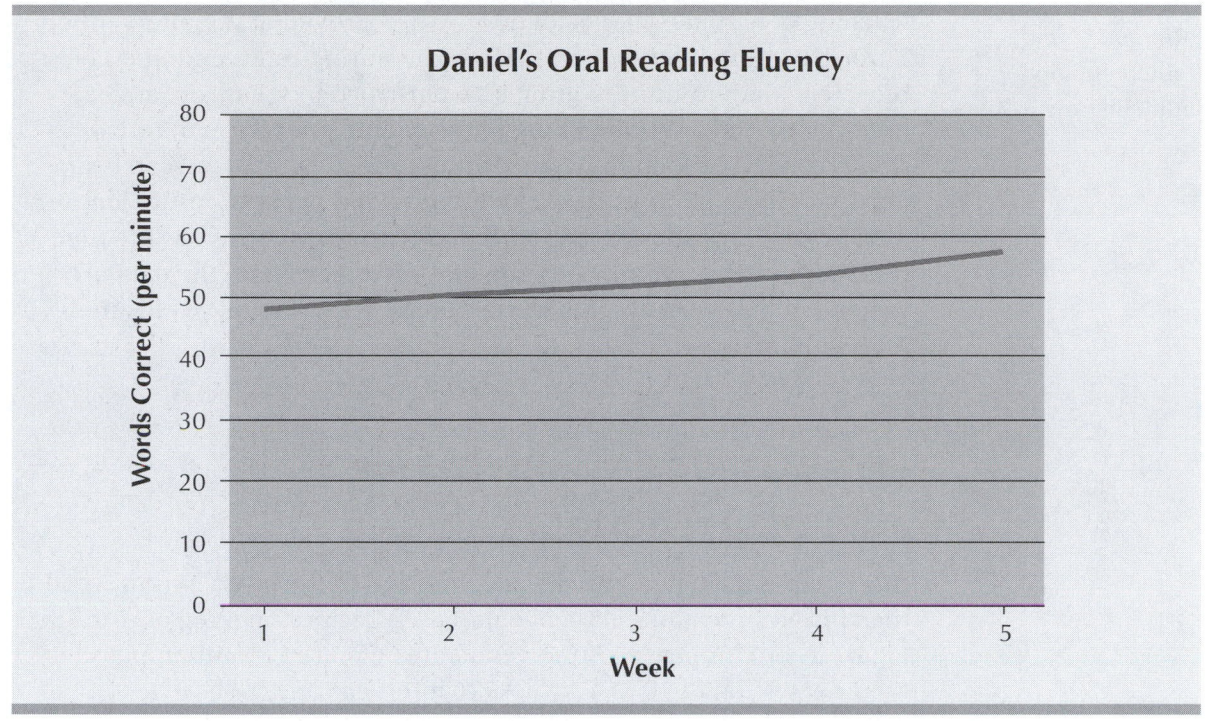

Daniel's Oral Reading Fluency

Instructional Planning: Modifying Instruction As Needed, Based on Data

Just as in the before-intervention phase after analyzing and reflecting on data, in the during-intervention phase it is time for planning and for modifying instruction. This sometimes means changing the grouping of students (e.g., Brenda), but more often it means small changes for individual learners (e.g., Ben). It is common to see one student in a group progressing more quickly than others; with careful planning, the teacher can continue to meet such a student's needs. For example, in Ms. Perry's group 2, Monica has been performing well on spelling words by adding the initial sound to the rime portion of the word; however, the rest of the group is still struggling with this skill. To meet all students' needs, Ms. Perry can have Monica spell the whole word at the same time as the others are working on adding the initial sound to spell the word. (See Figure 5.4, p. 87, for an example.)

Instruction: Using the CIM

With the next two weeks of intervention planned, it is time to return to teaching. Again, the CIM is followed when providing the intervention. Throughout the intervention session, the during-intervention cycle is repeated. Modifications to groups and instruction are made, and it is important to set a specified time for providing intervention. Intervention is conducted for a finite amount of time. Generally, research supports providing 10 to 12 weeks of intervention per session (O'Connor, 2007). Ms. Perry and Mr. Lee both decide to set 10 weeks as the time period for the intervention session and then reevaluate the data. At the end of the 10 weeks, Ms. Perry and Mr. Lee will follow the after-intervention phase.

Data-Based Decision Making after Intervention

After approximately 10 weeks, the duration of the intervention session, the after-intervention phase of data-based decision making begins. (See Figure 7.8.) This phase also serves as the before-intervention phase for the next session of 10 to 12 weeks of intervention.

Data Collection: Reassessing All Students

The after-intervention phase begins with reassessing all students, both those in intervention and those not in intervention, using the original screening measures. With these data, the growth of students in intervention can be compared to all students in the class, including those receiving only general classroom instruction. The after-intervention phase has two purposes. The first is to determine if students are making progress toward grade-level objectives at the same pace as others in the class. This is a time for teachers to evaluate if intervention is providing students with an added boost toward meeting grade-level objectives. In other words, are students responding to intervention? We would expect intervention students to make equal or greater growth than students not in intervention. The second purpose of this phase is to see if there are other students who were not receiving intervention but who now

FIGURE 7.8 **Data-Based Decision Making after Intervention**

135

Chapter Seven
The Data-Based
Decision-Making
Cycle

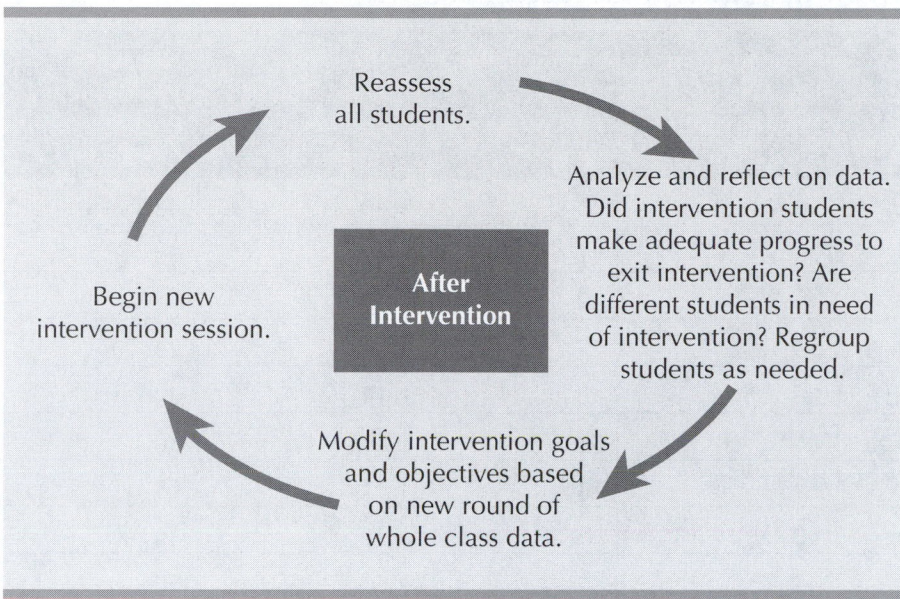

Reassess all students.

Analyze and reflect on data. Did intervention students make adequate progress to exit intervention? Are different students in need of intervention? Regroup students as needed.

After Intervention

Begin new intervention session.

Modify intervention goals and objectives based on new round of whole class data.

need it. This is the time for teachers to evaluate whether or not general classroom reading instruction is sufficient for those students not receiving intervention. Students who are not making adequate growth with general classroom reading instruction alone can begin intervention in the next session. Ms. Perry assessed her whole class again after the 10-week intervention session. The data she collected are shown in Table 7.6.

For students already identified with a learning disability, it is important to reassess, both on the instructional-level passages as well as on the grade-level passages, to determine how these students are progressing toward reading at grade level. When Mr. Lee reassessed Daniel, he scored a 60 on the first-grade-level passage, which was a major improvement after 10 weeks. Mr. Lee also administered the third-grade reading passage to determine how well Daniel was progressing toward grade-level reading. On the third-grade passage, Daniel read 17 words correctly out of 25 total words, which was also an improvement over the initial assessment.

TABLE 7.6 Ms. Perry's Class Data, Postintervention (about 10 weeks after initial screening)

Student Name	English Language Level	Segmentation Fluency, Preintervention (goal = 35)	Segmentation Fluency, Postintervention (goal = 35)	Nonsense Word Fluency, Preintervention (goal = 24)	Nonsense Word Fluency, Postintervention (goal = 50)
Candice[d]	Advanced	36	40	40	43
Michael	Proficient	35	41	42	50
Jacob	EO	38	39	45	55
Yvonne[a b]	Intermediate	15	25	8	25
Monica[a c]	Advanced	36	40	14	20
Lee[c]	Intermediate	35	36	24	30
Ben[a b]	EO	9	13	1	5
Alex[c]	Beginning	40	42	26	30
Tyler	EO	45	45	47	50
Leslie[a]	Beginning	37	42	18	53
Vanessa	EO	40	48	28	48
Isabel	Advanced	37	40	26	51
Humberto[a b]	Proficient	16	26	15	30
Marissa[d]	EO	43	45	30	40
Brenda[a d]	Advanced	14	42	19	45
Arianna	Intermediate	47	50	29	52
Kevin[a c]	EO	39	39	19	27
Vivian	Proficient	35	40	24	50
Francesca[d]	Proficient	41	45	24	41
Mario	Advanced	50	51	31	50
Kyle	EO	38	45	27	52
Ryana	EO	40	42	33	55
Juliana	Advanced	42	50	40	60

[a]Student received intervention.   [b]Student still below benchmark in both PA and alphabetic principle.
[c]Student below benchmark only in alphabetic principle.   [d]Student slightly below benchmark on alphabetic principle.
Note: EO = English only.

Analysis and Reflection:
Reviewing the Second-Round Data

The analysis and reflection in the after-intervention phase involves examining the second round of screening data to decide which students are still in need of intervention, which students have met their intervention goals and can be exited from intervention, and which students may need to be added to the intervention groups. After analyzing and reflecting on the data and observations, groups for intervention can be formed once again.

The data presented from Ms. Perry's class in Table 7.6 show that intervention is working for most students. Close examination of the data shows that all students except Ben have made growth. Humberto and Yvonne made a good amount of growth in PA (segmentation fluency) and sufficient growth in alphabetic principle (nonsense word fluency). Group 2 intervention students all made growth. Brenda and Leslie have both responded well to intervention and should be considered for exiting intervention. Monica and Kevin have made growth but did not meet the benchmarks; therefore, they should continue intervention for one more session (another 10 weeks of intervention). Analysis of students who were not in intervention shows that there are five students who did not meet benchmark on alphabetic principle. These data should be analyzed and reflected on to determine if these students should be added to intervention. After examining and reflecting on the data, Ms. Perry decides that, based on these students' scores and her observations, Lee and Alex should be added to intervention. She will monitor the other three students (Francesca, Marrissa, and Candice) over the next few weeks to make sure that they make progress and meet benchmark. She will also monitor Brenda, because although she made impressive growth, she is still not quite yet at the benchmark. (See Table 7.7.)

For students already identified with LD, Mr. Lee also analyzes the data after 10 weeks. Again, for many of these students, more data may need to be collected to plan for intervention. Mr. Lee analyzes the data from Daniel's reading fluency assessments and determines that Daniel has made excellent progress on the first-grade passages. He also made growth on the third-grade passage, but is still well below grade level. Mr. Lee will need to collect further data to create an intervention plan for Daniel for the next intervention session.

TABLE 7.7   Round 2 Intervention Groups

Progress monitor only: Francesca, Marissa, Candice, Brenda

Group 1, round 1	Group 1, round 2	Group 2, round 1	Group 2, round 2
Yvonne	Yvonne	Monica	Monica
Ben	Ben	Leslie	Kevin
Humberto	Humberto	Kevin	Lee
Brenda			Alex

Instructional Planning: Designing Another Intervention Session

After students have been selected for the second session of intervention and grouped according to data and observations, it is time to begin planning intervention. Again, if more information is needed to plan for instruction, further assessments should be administered. Much like planning in the before-intervention phase, the first step in planning is to write the goals for each group. Once goals are written, outlines for the first few weeks of intervention can be developed. Based on the data, Ms. Perry develops the following goals for group 1: "By the end of the 10-week intervention, students will segment and blend four- and five-phoneme words and will read and spell CVC words." Ms. Perry then uses the two-week planning template to plan for the first two weeks of intervention. She uses the same process for group 2.

Although Ms. Perry did not need to collect additional data, Mr. Lee needs more information to plan instruction for Daniel. Daniel made large growth on the first-grade passages during intervention, but the third-grade passages were still well above his instructional level. Mr. Lee chooses to administer the second-grade passage to determine if this is now Daniel's instructional level. Daniel reads 32 words correctly of 35 words. Although the passage is a bit difficult for Daniel, it is approximately at his instructional level. Based on Daniel's errors on the reading passages, it is evident that Daniel struggled with CVCe words and words with vowel combinations. To gain more information about the phonics skills Daniel has mastered and the ones he still needs to receive instruction in, Mr. Lee gives Daniel a phonics assessment. Daniel was able to accurately read CCVC, CVCC, and CCVCC words. The phonics test confirmed that Daniel also struggled with some CVCe words and words with vowel combinations. Mr. Lee set the following intervention goal for Daniel: "By the end of the 10-week intervention, Daniel will correctly read CVCe words, words with vowel combinations (ai, ea, ee, oa, oo, ou, and ow), and will increase his reading fluency on second-grade passages."

Instruction: Beginning a New Intervention Session

The final stage in the cycle is to begin a new intervention session and return to the during-intervention phase. Ms. Perry plans on meeting with group 1 each day for 30 minutes and meeting with group 2 for 20 minutes, three days each week. She plans to monitor progress weekly for all students in intervention group 1 and biweekly for students in intervention group 2, including the two students that were added to this session of intervention. Ms. Perry plans to assess the students who did not quite meet benchmark but are not in intervention each month to ensure they meet the benchmark. Mr. Lee meets with Daniel's intervention group for 45 minutes each day and monitors the progress of Daniel and the students in his group weekly. Both teachers will use the progress-monitoring data to make decisions about instruction and grouping of students.

This phase also brings the cycle full circle, and the cycle will continue this way throughout the year. As Ms. Perry continues to provide solid early reading intervention following the scope and sequence of ERPI and the CIM, she will have at most one to two students at the end of the year who are still struggling with these skills. Mr. Lee will continue to work with students who, like Daniel, are identified with LD and with other students who may not yet be identified but who are well below grade level in reading. Many of these students will need ongoing intervention to meet grade-level expectations. Mr. Lee will also work with teachers like Ms. Perry to support her in working with the one to two students in her class who are not responsive to intervention.

Summary

Data-based decision making is a cyclical process that provides a framework for using data to guide instruction. There are three phases in the data-based decision-making cycle: before, during, and after intervention. Each of the three phases has four stages: data collection, analysis and reflection, instructional planning, and instruction. Data collection involves assessing all students to determine which students are in need of intervention and also collecting progress-monitoring data on those students who are receiving intervention. During analysis and reflection, teachers examine individual student data to decide which students need intervention and to create intervention groups. During instructional planning, teachers more carefully look at individual student data to diagnose areas of need and then design intervention lessons accordingly. Finally, the intervention lessons are taught using the Core Intervention Model. The cycle then enters the next phase and moves through each of the stages again.

CHAPTER 8

Intervention in Your Classroom

Objectives

By the end of this chapter, the reader will be able to

1. State the five steps to implementing the Early Reading Project Intervention in his/her classroom

2. List materials needed to conduct intervention

3. Feel confident using the materials provided

4. Feel comfortable implementing the Early Reading Project Intervention with his/her students

Part One of this book provided a research base and rationale for providing early reading interventions to students at risk for reading difficulties. It also offered a deeper look at early reading research for English learners and students with learning disabilities. Part Two of this book built on the research and rationale provided in the first part to introduce the Early Reading Project Intervention (ERPI). The content and methods of intervention, as well as the data-based decision-making cycle for conducting intervention, were explored in detail. This final chapter provides the tools and materials for conducting ERPI in your classroom.

Designing Early Reading Intervention

Table 8.1 outlines the steps in designing an early reading intervention for your classroom.

Step 1. Make time.

The first step may be the hardest step—making time. Your school day is undoubtedly full, but time must be found for your struggling readers. Before getting started with assessment or intervention in your class, dedicate time in your day that will be set aside for administering assessments and/or providing intervention for those students who qualify for intervention. A 30-minute period of time should be set aside every day

TABLE 8.1   Steps and Materials Needed for Intervention

Step	What Is Needed
1. Make time.	Schedule template
2. Determine what the other students will be doing while you are conducting intervention.	Independent activities or activities that can be directed by instructional assistants, parents, and others.
3. Screen class and select students.	Assessments, data sheet
4. Conduct intervention.	Scope and sequence, lesson plans, staircases
5. Monitor progress and review student profiles.	Assessments, graph

or, at minimum, three days each week for assessment or intervention. During this 30-minute period, you will either be providing the intervention or administering assessments. At the beginning of the year during the first few weeks of school, use this time block to administer screening assessment to all of your students. After selecting students for intervention, use this time block to conduct intervention and collect weekly progress monitoring. (Remember, these assessments are generally quick and easy to administer; you will not spend a large amount of time with each student.) A sample weekly intervention schedule is shown in Appendix 8.1, and Appendix 8.2 has a blank schedule template. (Appendixes begin on p. 148.)

Step 2. Determine what students not in intervention will do.

Before beginning assessment or intervention, use a few weeks to establish rules and routines for this time. Most teachers try to implement independent working time for students not in intervention. Taking the time to teach the students how to use each other as resources if they have questions and what to do when they finish their activity will allow you to focus on intervention once you get started. Also, soliciting parent help or even the help of an older student can be of assistance during this time. *What Are the Other Kids Doing While You Teach Small Group?* (Marriot, 1997) and *Words Their Way* (Bear, Invernize, Templeton & Johnston, 2003) are excellent resources for activities that students can do while you are conducting intervention with a small group.

Step 3. Screen the class and select students for intervention.

At first glance, screening all students may appear to be an overwhelming task, but intervention cannot begin without it. All students must be screened, but to save some time, evaluate all the assessments you are asked to administer to see if there is any overlap and if some can be eliminated. For example, if you have two measures that assess phonological awareness, look at them closely to see which will give you the most information about students' skill levels and on the errors they make.

Prior to screening all of your students, it is a good idea to review the assessments and ensure that you have all the assessment materials. If your school does not have a screening measure that covers early reading skills, you will need to choose one (see the resources listed in Box 7.1, pp. 116–117). You will need to have enough copies of the materials for all students in your class. Once you have completed the screening, use the data form in Appendix 8.3 to record all data. If you prefer, you may instead create an electronic table in Excel to enter data, or you may have access to an electronic database at your school. The most important factor is to make your data accessible and usable. In order to make intervention effective, the data must be meaningful to you as a teacher, so use materials that work with your strengths. If you do not like computers, make a folder for each student and include a table and graph to show progress. You will want to be able to quickly and easily look at student results to evaluate growth. You will also want to take time to analyze student response sheets from the assessments to look for patterns showing strengths and areas of need for your intervention students. This step helps in focusing the intervention on each student's specific needs. You may use the table template in Appendix 8.4 to record your analysis.

Step 4. Conduct intervention.

Before starting intervention, the goals and objectives for the students in your group need to be set. These goals and objectives help to pinpoint where to begin intervention, based on the scope and sequence provided in Chapter 5. The scope and sequence is provided again in Appendix 8.5, with more detail, including a full list of related activities. After you become familiar with these activities, you will be able to adapt these activities to meet your students' needs. When choosing activities, it is important to remember that they must be connected to the student's goals and objectives. If you choose a PA activity that is focusing on segmenting three phonemes, but your student is only able to segment the onset, be prepared to simplify. Such resources as the following can be helpful in planning intervention activities: *Interventions for Reading Success* (Haager, Dimino & Windmuller, 2007), the Making Words series (Cunningham & Hall, 2001), and *Phonics They Use* (Cunningham, 2004).

Appendixes 8.6 and 8.7 provide two different lesson planning templates that can be used to develop intervention lessons. The lesson plan forms are developed to follow the Core Intervention Model of instruction presented in Chapter 6. Appendix 8.8 is a checklist from the ERPI to assist you meeting the six principles of the CIM. The correction procedures included as part of the CIM are some of the most important aspects of the ERPI. Box 8.1 provides four examples of the staircase approach for different goals and objectives to help guide the use of the CIM. We recommend writing out staircases for a few of your intervention activities prior to beginning intervention. After working with the staircase, it will become second nature, but many teachers have reported that it is difficult implement without preparation at the beginning.

Step 5. Monitor progress and review student profiles.

The ERPI does not stop with providing instruction. Progress monitoring and review of student performance are necessary to ensure the intervention is successful and to provide information for making modifications to the intervention. Recording student progress in an Excel

Box 8.1

Box 8.1

Examples of the Staircase Approach

Blending three-phoneme words orally—"Guess My Word"

1. Original prompt: "Guess my word, /l/-/o/-/g/."

2. Onset-rime blend: "Guess my word, /l/-/og/."

3. Yes/no question: "Is my word *log*?"

4. Telling the answer: "My word is *log*."

5. Say and repeat: "Log. Say, *log*."

Tapping phonemes— three-phoneme words

1. Original prompt: "Tap all the sounds you hear in *lake*."

2. Onset-rime tap: "Tap two sounds you hear in *lake*." As you say this, remove one of the placeholders so that only two are there.

3. First sound tap: "Tap the first sound you hear in *lake*." As you say, this remove one of the placeholders so that only one is there.

4. Yes/no question: "Lake. Do you hear /l/-/a/-/ke/?" Tap each sound on students' placeholders as you say the sounds.

5. Telling the answer: "The sounds in *lake* are /l/-/a/-/ke/."

6. Say and repeat: "/L/-/a/-/ke/. Say, /l/-/a/-/ke/."

Spelling CVC words

1. Original prompt: "Spell the word *cup*."

2. Missing or wrong letter: "What sounds do you hear in *cup*? What letter makes the /c/ sound?"

3. Segmenting: "Tap the sounds in *cup*."

4. Yes/no question: "Cup. Do you hear /c/-/u/-/p/?" Tap each sound for the students as you say the sounds. "Does this spell *cup*?" Write the word on the board for the students.

5. Telling the answer: "The sounds in *cup* are /c/-/u/-/p/. This spells *cup*." Point to what you wrote.

6. Say/do and repeat: "/C/-/u/-/p/. Say, /c/-/u/-/p/. Write *cup*." Have students copy your spelling.

Reading more difficult words in text

1. Original prompt: "Read the sentence: *The kids ran fast.*"

2. Prompt for a reread: "Put your finger on the word that begins with *f*. Read the word again."

3. Prompt for specific part decoding incorrectly: "What sound do these letters make—/st/?"

4. Telling the answer: "*St* makes the sound /st/."

5. Say and have student repeat: "The word is *fast*. Read it."

Note: Do not use the staircase for each word the student decodes incorrectly. Choose to use correction procedures on the intervention target skill, in this case, words with consonant blends. If the student read *kids* incorrectly, then tell the word and have the student repeat and reread the sentence.

database or in folders containing your handwritten charts and graphs are both effective ways to manage the student data. The template in Appendix 8.9 can be used if you choose to use student folders. Your school may have a database they wish you use for entering student data. Graphs showing individual student data are a visual way to represent how the student is doing. These graphs, along with your analysis of the data, are helpful to have for meetings with parents, grade-level planning meetings, and Student Study Team meetings. These graphs can also be highly motivating for both the students and you; after all, there is nothing better than having evidence that your and their hard work is paying off.

Conclusion

We hope that the materials provided will help you begin using the ERPI in your classroom. The ERPI is not like a typical curriculum that you pick up and begin implementing; it is a guide for developing and implementing intervention in your classroom. The scope and sequence is laid out. The methods are concrete, and the process of using data to guide your instruction is systematic. However, the rate at which you move through the scope and sequence, the activities you choose, and the pace of each lesson are determined by the individual learners sitting in front of you.

Appendix 8.1
Sample Weekly Schedule

	Monday	Tuesday	Wednesday	Thursday	Friday
8:00–9:00	Language arts whole class instruction				
9:00–9:30	Intervention Group 1	Intervention Group 1	Intervention Group 1	Intervention Group 1	Assessment
9:30–10:00	Intervention Group 2	Library	Intervention Group 2	Intervention Group 2	Assessment
10:00–10:15	Recess				
10:15–11:00	Small group reading (students not in intervention)				
11:00–11:30	Writing instruction/writers workshop				
11:30–12:00	English language development (Students not needing ELD continue writers workshop)				
12:00–12:30	Lunch				
12:30–1:30	Math				
1:30–2:00	Science	Social Studies	Science	Social Studies	Science
2:00–2:30	PE	PE	Music	PE	PE

Appendix 8.2
Weekly Schedule Template

	Monday	Tuesday	Wednesday	Thursday	Friday
8:00–8:30					
8:30–9:00					
9:00–9:30					
9:30–10:00					
10:00–10:30					
10:30-11:00					
11:00-11:30					
11:30–12:00					
12:00–12:30					
12:30–1:00					
1:00–1:30					
1:30-2:00					
2:00-2:30					
2:30–3:00					

Appendix 8.3
Data Form for Recording Screening Data

Student Name	Assessment Name	Assessment Name	Assessment Name

Group 1:

Group 2:

Appendix 8.4
Data Analysis Form for Intervention Students

Student name _____

Assessment Name	Score	Benchmark Score	Strengths Found in Assessment	Needs Found in Assessment

Student name _____

Assessment Name	Score	Benchmark Score	Strengths Found in Assessment	Needs Found in Assessment

Appendix 8.5

Scope and Sequence of Intervention and Intervention Activities

I. Scope and Sequence Table

Phonological Awareness *Rime/Onset/Blending/Segmentation*	Phonics *Letter-Sound Relationships*	Phonics *Decoding/Spelling*
1. Onset: Beginning sound identification 2. Onset: Orally matching beginning sounds with pictures 3. Rime: Orally matching rhyming words with pictures	1. Letter-sound match	
4. Blending: Onset-rime blending orally 5. Segmenting: Onset-rime tap		
6. Blending: 3-phoneme words orally 7. Segmenting: Tapping phonemes, 3-phoneme words	2. Letter-sound flashcards	
8. Blending: 4- to 5-phoneme words 9. Onset: Producing a word that begins with the same beginning sound 10. Segmenting: Manipulating first letter in words orally		1. Spelling CVC words given the rime portion of the word (-at, spell *cat*) and reading the CVC words
11. Segmenting: Sound counting CVC words 12. Segmenting: Manipulating final sounds orally 13. Segmenting: Manipulating middle sounds orally 14. Rime: Producing a word that rhymes		2. Spelling VC and CVC words and reading the words
		3. Manipulating sounds (first, final, or middle) to spell new CVC words to read 4. Reading CVC words in text
		5. Reading more difficult words[a] 6. Spelling more difficult words[a] 7. Manipulating sounds to spell more difficult words[a] 8. Reading more difficult words[a] in text

[a]More difficult words are all words that are taught after CVC words, including CVCC, CCVC, CCCVC, CVCe, CVVC, CCVVC, and so on, and also multisyllabic words.

II. Intervention Activities

A. Letter Knowledge

1. Letter-sound matching

Materials: Letter cards

a. Choose 6 to 10 letters that students have difficulty with.

b. Place cards face up in front of students.

c. **Model:** "I am going to say the sound of the letter, and I want you to find the letter that makes that sound. Say, /d/. What letter makes the sound /d/?" Model finding the *d* letter card.

d. **Guided practice:** Follow the same procedures; have students do a few letters with you.

e. **Practice:** Call out several letter sounds, using group and individual responding.

2. Letter-sound flashcards

Materials: Letter cards

a. Choose 10 to 15 letters that students have difficulty with and/or will be used in the lesson for the day.

b. **Model:** "I am going to show a letter, and I want you to say the name of it and then tell me the sound. Watch." Show the letter *c*. Say, "/c/."

c. **Guided practice:** Follow the same procedures; have students do a few letters with you.

d. **Independent practice:** Show several letters, using group and individual responding.

B. Phonological Awareness

1. Beginning-sound identification

Materials: Picture cards of words with the same sound (2 to 5 different beginning sounds, depending on student level)

a. Choose 2 to 5 different beginning sounds, depending on student level.

b. **Model:** "I am going to show you a picture and say the word. Then I want you to tell me the first sound you hear in the word. Watch me." Show picture, i.e., cat. Say, "/c/—*cat.*"

c. **Guided practice:** Follow the same procedures; have students do a few pictures with you.

d. **Independent practice:** Show several pictures, using group and individual responding.

2. **Orally matching beginning sounds with pictures**

   Materials: Picture cards with words that start with the same beginning sounds (with several different initial sounds)

   a. Select a series of picture cards that have the same beginning sound and a few that do not.

   b. Go through each of the pictures you will use, naming them. (This is particularly important for EL students, who may not have words in English.)

   c. Model: Show students a picture and say name of the picture (i.e., *dog*). Put another picture down and say the name (i.e., *duck*). "Say it: *dog—duck*." Ask, "Does *dog* start with the same sound as *duck*?" Say, "Yes, *dog* does start with the same sound as *duck*, *dog—duck*."

   d. Guided practice: Do this with the students with 3 or 4 more sets of pictures, using both words that have the same beginning sound and those that do not (i.e., *dog—run*).

   e. Practice: Show several picture sets (words that rhyme and words that do not), using group and individual responding.

   - Once students are able to determine if words start with the same beginning sound with only one option, add another picture and ask, for example, "Does *dog* start with the same sound as *duck* or *bell*?"

   - Other variations are to place 3 or 4 pictures in front of students and have them choose the words from the group that start the same, having either one word that does not start the same (i.e., *cat, cut, bus, cap*) or two words that do not start the same (i.e., *cat, fish, cut, bus*).

   - In the early stages of developing rime identification, students have difficulty distinguishing between words that have any of the same sounds, so initially begin with words that are very different if they do not rhyme (i.e., choose *cat—fin* over *cat—cup* or *cat—nut*).

3. **Orally rhyming with pictures**

   Materials: Picture cards with rhyming words (with several different rime patterns)

   a. Select a series of picture cards that rhyme and a few from other rhyme patterns that do not.

   b. Go through each of the pictures you will use naming them. (This is particularly important for EL students who may not have words in English.)

c. **Model:** Show students one picture and say name of the picture (i.e., *dog*). Put another picture down and say the name (i.e., *log*). Say, "*Dog—log.*" Ask, "Does *dog* rhyme with *log*?" Say, "Yes; *dog* does rhyme with *log*; *dog—log.*"

d. **Guided practice:** Do this with the students with 3 or 4 more sets of pictures, using both words that rhyme and those that do not (i.e., *cat—pen*).

e. **Practice:** Show several picture sets (words that rhyme and words that do not), using group and individual responding.

   • Once students are able to determine if words rhyme with only one option, add another picture and ask, for example, "Does *dog* rhyme with *log* or *boat*?"

   • Other variations are to place 3 or 4 pictures in front of students and have them choose the words from the group that rhyme, having either one word that does not rhyme (i.e., *cat, rat, cut, bat*) or two words that do not rhyme (i.e., *cat, fin, cut, bat*).

   • In the early stages of developing rime identification, students have difficulty distinguishing between words that have any of the same sounds, so initially begin with words that are very different if they do not rhyme (i.e., choose *cat—fin* over *cat— cup* or *cat—nut*).

4. **Onset rime blending orally—"Guess My Word"**

Materials: Small paper bag with picture cards with CVC, CVCe, or CVVC words

a. Tell students, "We will be playing the game Guess My Word."

b. **Model:** "I am going to tell you the sounds of the word. Then you will try to guess my word." Say, "If I say, 'Guess my word—/d/-/og/,' you say *dog*."

c. **Guided practice:** Follow the same procedures. Have students guess the word, and you repeat the correct answer.

d. **Practice:** Do this several times using group and individual re-sponding.

   • This activity can be done without pictures and/or the grab bag and just by saying the onset rime in words.

5. **Onset rime tapping**

Materials: 2 placeholders per student, word list from 2 to 3 word families (CVC words)

a. Give each student 2 placeholders and place them in front of them.

b. Tell students, "We will be working on hearing the sound in words. When we hear the sounds, we will tap them."

c. Model: "Watch me. *cat*, /c/-/at/." As you say this, tap on your placeholders.

d. Guided practice: Have students practice /c/-/at/. Students tap placeholders for the onset and rime—/c/-/at/. Do several more words with the students.

e. Practice: Do several more words, using group and individual responding.

6. **Blending 3-phoneme words orally—"Guess My Word"**

   Materials: Small paper bag with picture cards with CVC, CVCe, or CVVC words

   a. Tell students, "We will be playing the game Guess My Word."

   b. Model: "I am going to tell you the sounds of the word. Then you will try to guess my word." Say, "If I say, 'Guess my word— /d/-/o/-/g/,' you say *dog*."

   c. Guided practice: Follow the same procedures. Have students guess the word, and you repeat the correct answer.

   d. Practice: Do this several times, using group and individual responding.

   • This activity can be done without pictures and/or the grab bag and just by saying all three sounds in the word.

7. **Tapping phonemes—3-phoneme words**

   Materials: 3 placeholders per student, word list from 2 to 3 word families (CVC words)

   a. Give each student 3 placeholders and place in front of them.

   b. Tell students, "We will be working on hearing the sounds in words. When we hear the sounds, we will tap them."

   c. Model: "Watch me. *Cat*—/c/-/a/-/t/." As you say this, tap on your placeholders.

   d. Guided practice: Have the students practice /c/-/a/-/t/. Have students tap placeholders for each sound—/c/-/a/-/t/. Do several more words with the students.

   e. Practice: Do several more words, using group and individual responding.

8. **Blending 4 to 5 phonemes orally—"Guess My Word"**

Materials: Small paper bag, pictures card with CVCC, CVCC, CCVCC, CVVCC, and CCVVC words

a. Tell students, "We will be playing the game Guess My Word."

b. **Model:** "I am going to tell you the sounds of the word. Then you will try to guess my word." Say, "If I say 'Guess my word—/s/-/n/-/a/-/k/-/e/,' you say *snake.*"

c. **Guided practice:** Follow the same procedures. Have students guess the word, and you repeat the correct answer.

d. **Practice:** Do this several times, using group and individual responding.

   • This activity can be done without pictures and/or the grab bag and just by saying all 4 to 5 sounds in the word.

9. **Producing a word that starts with the same beginning sound**

Materials: Picture cards, white board, marker

a. Tell students, "I am going to say a word, and then I want you to tell me a word that starts with the same beginning sound."

b. **Model:** "I want to think of a word that starts with the same sound as *man.*" Use a picture for EL support. "*Man*—/m/-/an/. I hear the /m/ sound at the beginning. What is another word I can think of that starts with the /m/ sound? *Mouse* starts with the /m/ sound." Write the words on the board, and check to see if students hear the same sound and then if they start with the same letter.

c. **Guided practice:** Do several words with the students, writing each response on the board and underlining the first letter to illustrate that, in most cases, words that start with the same sound also start with the same letter.

d. **Practice:** Do this several times, using group and individual responding.

10. **Manipulating the first sound in the word orally**

Materials: Word lists from several word families (3-phoneme words), segmenting placeholders

a. Tell students, "I am going to say a word and then tell you to take off the first sound and add a new sound to make a new word."

b. **Model:** "Listen, *cat.* If I take off the /c/ in *cat* and add a /b/, what word do I get?" Tap the sounds in *cat;* say /c/-/a/-/t/; then move the first placeholder and say, "Take off the /c/." Put it back and say, "Put on /b/." Tap and say, "/B/-/a/-/t/. I get *bat.*"

c. **Guided practice:** Do several words with the students, using a few different word families.

d. Practice: Do this several more times, using different word families and using group and individual responding.

11. Sound counting CVC words

Materials: Word list of 2 to 3 word families (CVC words)

a. Tell students, "You will be counting how many sounds you hear in each word. This will help when you want to spell a word."

b. Model: "Watch me, *cat*—/c/-/a/-/t/." As you say this, put up a finger for each sound. Say, "I heard 3 sounds."

c. Guided practice: Have students practice cat. Students hold up one finger for each of the three sounds, then say, "3 sounds." Model a few more words and have students practice.

d. Practice: Say a word and have students count the phonemes; repeat with several words.

12. Manipulating the final sound in words

Materials: Word lists with same initial and middle sounds (3-phoneme words), segmenting placeholders

a. Tell students, "I am going to say a word and then tell you to take off the last sound and add a new sound to make a new word."

b. Model: "Listen, *cat*. If I take off the /t/ in *cat* and add a /p/, what word do I get?" Tap the sounds in *cat*; say, "/c/-/a/-/t/"; then move the last placeholder and say, "Take off the /t/." Put it back and say, "Put on /p/." Tap and say, "/C/-/a/-/p/. I get *cap*."

c. Guided practice: Do several words with the students, using a few different word families.

d. Practice: Do this several more times, using different word families and using group and individual responding.

13. Manipulating the middle sound in words

Materials: Word lists from several words with same initial and final sounds (3-phoneme words), segmenting placeholders

a. Tell students, "I am going to say a word and then tell you to take out the middle sound and add a new sound to make a new word."

b. Model: "Listen, *cat*. If I take out the /a/ in *cat*, and put in a /u/, what word do I get?" Tap the sounds in *cat*; say "/c/-/a/-/t/"; then move the middle placeholder and say, "Take out the /a/." Put it back and say, "Put in /u/." Tap and say, "/C/-/u/-/t/. I get *cut*."

c. Guided practice: Do several words with the students, using a few different word families.

d. Practice: Do this several more times, using different word families and using group and individual responding.

14. **Producing a word that rhymes**

   Materials: Picture cards, white board, marker

   a. Tell students, "I am going to say a word and then I want you to tell me a word that rhymes with the word."

   b. Model: "I want to think of a word that rhymes with *man*." Use a picture for EL support. "*Man*—/m/-/an/. I hear /an/ at the end. What is another word I can think of that has the /an/ sound and rhymes? /F/-/an/. *Fan* has the /an/ sound. *Fan—man*; *fan—man*. Those sound the same. They rhyme." Write the words on the board and underline the ending sound to illustrate the letter patterns.

   c. Guided practice: Do several words with the students, writing each response on the board and underlining the first letter to illustrate that, in most cases, words have the same letter patterns.

   d. Practice: Do this several times, using group and individual responding.

C. Phonics: Decoding and Spelling

1. **Spelling CVC words given the rime portion of the word and reading the CVC words**

   Materials: Large post-its and small post-its (two different colors); prepare large post-it notes with 2 to 3 rime endings, prepare small post-its with consonants that form words with the rimes. For example:

   a. Review the consonant sounds that you will use.

   b. Start with one rime. Read the rime to students. "/A/-/t/ spells /at/. We are going to make words that end in -at. These words rhyme."

   c. Model: Say, "I want to make the word *cat*. I am going to think of what sound I hear at the beginning of *cat*. /C/-/c/—/cat/."

   d. Guided practice: Have students take off the *c* and now make the word *bat*. Do it with them. Do several more examples with the students.

e. Practice: Do several more words, using group and individual responding. For individual responding, give each student a different word; they can all be working on their words at the same time.

2. **Spelling CV and CVC words and reading the words**

Materials: Pencils, small post-its, index cards (or whiteboards, markers), list of CVC words

a. Tell students that you will be practicing spelling and reading words today.

b. Model: "I want to spell the word *sad. /S/-/a/-/d/.*" Count the sounds using finger counting. "I am going to put down a post-it for each sound I counted—3." Write the letters on the post-its—*s-a-d.* "Now I going to write the word on my index card all together." Write *sad* as a whole word. "I am going to read my word—*sad.*"

c. Guided practice: Do several words with the students.

d. Practice: Do several more words, using group and individual responding. For individual responding, give each student a different word; they can work on their words at the same time.

e. Before concluding the lesson, go back to all index cards and have students read them using individual and group responding.

3. **Manipulating sounds to spell new CVC words to read**

Materials: Post-its, pencils, index cards (or whiteboards, markers), list of CVC words from several word families

a. Tell students, "We will be practicing spelling and reading words."

b. Model: "I want to spell the word *sad. /S/-/a/-/d/.*" Count the sounds using finger counting. "I am going to put down a post-it for each sound I counted—3." Write the letters on the post-its—*s-a-d.* "Now I want to change one sound in *sad* and make *mad—/m/-/a/-/d/.* What letter do I need to change to /m/-/a/-/d/? I need to have the /m/ sound. What letter makes the /m/ sound? *M* makes the /m/ sound." As you say this, remove the post-it with the *s* and get a new post-it and put an *m* on it. Say, "Let me tap to make sure I spelled the new word *mad—-/m/-/a/-/d/.*" Tap each sound on the post-it with the letter. "Now I going to write the word on my index card all together." Write *mad* as a whole word. "I am going to read my word—*mad.*"

c. Guided practice: Do several words with the students.

d. Practice: Do several more words, using group and individual responding. For individual responding, give each student a different word; they can all work on their words at the same time.

e. Before concluding the lesson, go back to all the index cards and have students read them, using individual and group responding.

4. **Reading words in text**

Materials: Short sentences or passages with CVC words that have been taught or are in the current lesson

a. Tell students, "We will be practicing reading words in sentences or short stories."

b. **Model:** Read the sentence or passage aloud to students.

c. **Guided practice:** Have students read the passage with you a few times.

d. **Practice:** Have each student read the passage aloud, either to the whole group or to you individually, while the other students practice quietly.

5. **Reading more difficult words (words with consonant blends, CVCe, and words with vowel combinations)**

Materials: Pencils , index cards (or whiteboards, markers), list of words with patterns you are working on (see chart for order of teaching at the beginning of this appendix)

a. Tell students, "We will be practicing reading words today."

b. **Model:** Tell the letters to write the word *brag*. Write *b-r-a-g*. Model writing this on an index card or the whiteboard. Ask, "What are the sounds? Sound it out—/b/-/r/-/a/-/g/. Read it— *brag*."

c. Have the students practice a few words with you.

d. Tell students the spelling of the word and then have them sound out the words and then read them.

6. **Spelling more difficult words and reading the words**

Materials: Pencils, small post-its, index cards (or whiteboards, markers), list of words (choose from 4- to 5-phoneme words with consonant blends and short vowels [CVCC, CCVC, CCCVC], words with long vowel and silent *e* [CVCe], words with vowel combinations, or multisyllabic words, depending on level of the students). The following is one example with vowel combinations:

a. Tell the students, "We will be practicing spelling and reading words with the /oo/ sound, like in the word *book*."

b. **Model:** "I want to spell the word *book*—/b-/oo/-/k/." Count the sounds, using finger counting. "I am going to put down a post-it for each sound I counted—3. I am going to write the letters on the post-its—*b-oo-k*." Write *b*. "What sound goes /oo/? It's *oo*."

Write *oo*. Write *k*. "Now I going to write the word on my index card all together." Write *book* as a whole word. "I am going to read my word—*book*."

c. **Guided practice:** Do several words with the students.

d. **Practice:** Do several more words using group and individual responding. For individual responding, give each student a different word; they can all work on their words at the same time.

e. Before concluding the lesson, go back to all index cards and have the students read them, using individual and group responding.

7. **Manipulating sounds to spell more difficult words to read**

Materials: Pencils, index cards (or whiteboard, markers), list of words with patterns

a. Tell the students, "We will be practicing reading words today."

b. **Model:** Tell the letters to write a word. Write *b-r-a-g*. Model writing this word on an index card or the whiteboard. "What are the sounds? Sound it out—/b/-/r/-/a/-/g/. Read it—*brag*. Now I want you to change the *b* to a *d*. Read the new word."

c. **Guided practice:** Have the students practice a few words with you, altering the letter(s) you manipulate: beginning, end, middle.

d. **Practice:** Do several more words, using group and individual responding. For individual responding, give each student a different word; they can work on their words at the same time.

8. **Reading more difficult words in text**

Materials: Short sentences or passages with more difficult words that have been taught or are in the current lesson

a. Tell the students, "We will be practicing reading words in sentences or short stories."

b. **Model:** Read the sentence or passage aloud to students.

c. **Guided practice:** Have the students read passage with you a few times.

d. **Practice:** Have each student read the passage aloud, either to the whole group or to you individually while the other students practice quietly.

Appendix 8.6
Daily Lesson Plan Template

Lesson Plan

Date: **Lesson #:** **Group: 1** **Students present:**	**Materials:** **Minutes of instruction:**

Objective:

Reviewed skills:

Word families:

Lesson

Activity 1:

Activity 2:

Activity 3:

Appendix 8.7
Biweekly Lesson Planning Template

Objective 1:				
Objective 2:				
Day				**Notes**
Monday *Target skill:*				
Wednesday *Target skill:*				
Friday *Target skill:*				
Monday *Target skill:*				
Wednesday *Target skill:*				
Friday **ASSESS!!!!**	Notes for next sessions:			

Appendix 8.8
Core Intervention Model Checklist

Group_____

Date_____

Component	Present	Absent	Notes
1. Have 3 to 4 students in the group.			
2. State the objective for the activity.			
3. Model each activity			
4. Break activities down into steps for students.			
5. Provide guided practice.			
6. Praise students often for correct responses.			
7. Give students many opportunities to respond.			
8. Provide corrective feedback using staircase.			
9. Teach to mastery.			
Percent of components present and absent			

Appendix 8.9
Individual Student Data Template

Student name _____

Assessment name: _____

Time Point	Score (correct sounds/ words per minute)	Observations/Comments
1		
2		
3		
4		
5		
6		
7		
8		
9		
10		

Assessment name: _____

Acronym Code List

Acronym	Full Term
CBM	curriculum-based measurement
CIM	Core Intervention Model
CVC, CVCC, CCVC, CVCe	used to describe types of words: C = consonant, V = vowel, *e* = silent *e*
DBDM	data-based decision making
DIBELS	Dynamic Indicators of Basic Early Literacy Skills
ELD	English language development
ELs	English learners
ERPI	Early Reading Project Intervention
IDEIA	Individuals with Disabilities Education Improvement Act (2004)
IEP	Individual Education Plan (or Program)
LD	learning disabilities
NRP	National Reading Panel
PA	phonological awareness
RTI	response to intervention

Glossary

alphabetic principle   understanding how written letters are connected to sounds: letter-sound knowledge, sounding out words, and reading connected text

blending   joining individual phonemes together with pronunciation to access a word; the opposite of segmenting.

cognitive capacity   the amount of space available for processing information

comprehension   the ability to make meaning of text (NRP, 2000)

context-reduced material   language, written or spoken, where few clues to the meaning are given

Core Intervention Model   a model for providing direct, systematic intervention for struggling learners, derived from research projects La Patera and ERP

correction staircase   a correction procedure designed to lead a student to the correct answer; this procedure systematically reduces the demand placed on the student so that the student can respond correctly

cross-linguistic transfer   knowledge or skills known in one's stronger language that can be accessed and used in one's second language

curriculum-based measurement   an effective assessment tool for monitoring student progress during instruction

data-based decision making   the process of using data to guide instruction; DBD includes prescreening, ongoing progress monitoring, and final assessment

decoding   translating printed text into the sounds of language

differentiate   the process of individualizing teaching to meet the unique needs of each student

fluency   the ability to complete a task accurately and quickly

general classroom reading instruction   effective classroom instruction based on grade-level standards

goals   the knowledge or skills that a teaching unit aims to teach

guided practice   students work on new skills while being supported by the teacher

independent practice   students work without direct teacher support on skills that have been learned in order to achieve mastery

individual differences   unique characteristics and behaviors that make every person different than another

instructional reading level   the level of reading material that should be used for instructional purposes; calculated by dividing the number of words read during a one-minute oral-reading-fluency probe by the number of words read correctly (text material in which a student attains a 94 to 96 percent is instructional)

intervention session   a preset time span for providing intervention prior to final evaluation, typically 10 weeks

interventions   instruction designed to meet the individual needs of learners struggling in a specific area

modeling   when a teacher demonstrates a new skill as a means of teaching the new skill to students

objectives   the knowledge or skills that a teaching lesson aims to teach; objectives focus on more specific skills and knowledge than goals

onset   the first sound(s) in a word, either an individual sound or blend

phoneme   the smallest unit in the sound system of language that serves to distinguish meaning

phonemic awareness   the understanding that words are made up of individual sounds, or phonemes

phonics instruction   teaching students the relationship between letters and the sounds they spell

phonological awareness   an awareness of the sounds in spoken language: words are made up of sounds, words are part of sentences, and syllables are part of words

progress monitoring   assessing student progress during instruction to evaluate the effectiveness of instruction; generally done on a weekly or biweekly basis

response to intervention   a three-tier instructional model designed to provide effective intervention to struggling students

rime   the part of the word or syllable that includes the vowel and the following consonants; identifying, producing, and manipulating the rime of words is a phonological awareness skill

screening assessment   a tool used to evaluate students' current knowledge in a given area; typically given prior to beginning instruction or intervention with the goal of basing instruction on what the student needs to learn

segmentation   the partitioning of sounds, syllables, or words into individual parts (the opposite of blending)

system of least prompts   a term from behavior theory that states that only the number of prompts necessary for a student to get to a correct response should be provided

target skill   focus skills for the intervention; the area of need for the student that is based on data

vocabulary   the understanding of the meaning of individual words, both orally and when reading (NRP, 2000)

working memory   a theoretical concept that represents the temporary storage and processing of information; used when a person is actively processing information before the information is transferred to long-term memory or lost

References

Abedi, J. (2002). Standardized achievement tests and English language learners: Psychometric issues. *Educational Assessment, 8,* 231–257.

Adams, G., & Carnine, D. (2003). Direct instruction. In H. L. Swanson, K. R. Harris & S. Graham (Eds.), *Handbook of learning disabilities* (pp. 403–416). New York: Guilford Press.

Adams, G. L., & Engelmann, S. (1996). Research on direct instruction: 25 years beyond DISTAR. Portland: Educational Achievement Systems.

Adams, L. F. (1990). Teaching text structure strategy: The acquisition and effectiveness of a strategy to increase textbook comprehension. *Dissertation Abstracts International, 50*(9-A), 28–46.

August, D., & Hakuta, K. (Eds.). (1997). *Improving schooling for language-minority children: A research agenda.* Washington, DC: National Academy Press.

August, D., & Shanahan, T. (Eds.). *Developing literacy in second language learners: Report of the National Literacy Panel on Language-Minority Children and Youth* (pp. 415–488). Mahwah, NJ: Erlbaum.

Baddeley, A. (1986). *Working memory.* Oxford: Oxford University Press.

Baddeley, A. D., & Hitch, G. (1974). Working memory. In G. H. Bower (Ed.), *The psychology of learning and motivation* (pp. 47–90). New York: Academic Press.

Baker, K. (1998). Structured English immersion: Breakthrough in teaching limited-English-proficient students. *Phi Delta Kappan, 79,* 199–203.

Baker, S., & Gersten, R. (1997). *Exploratory meta-analysis of instructional practices for English-language learners.* (Tech Rep. No. 97–01). Eugene, OR: Eugene Research Institute.

Bear, D. R., Invernizzi, M., Templeton, S., & Johnston, F. (2003). *Words their way.* Upper Saddle River, NJ: Prentice Hall.

Beck, I. L., McKeown, M. G., & Kucan, L. (2002). *Bringing words to life: Robust vocabulary instruction.* New York: Guilford Press.

Bialystok, E. (2007). Acquisition of literacy in bilingual children: A framework for research. *Language Learning, 57*(1), 45–77.

Bialystok, E., & Hakuta, K. (1994). *In other words.* New York: Basic Books.

Biemiller, A. (2003). Vocabulary: Needed if more children are to read well. *Reading Psychology, 24*(3–4), 323–335.

Biemiller, A., & Slonim, N. (2001). Estimating root word vocabulary growth in normative and advantaged populations: Evidence for a common sequence of vocabulary acquisition. *Journal of Educational Psychology, 93*(3), 498–520.

Brown, I. S., & Felton, R. H. (1990). Effects of instruction on beginning reading skills on children at risk for reading disability. *Reading and Writing: An Interdisciplinary Journal, 2*(3), 223–241.

Bruner, J. (1960). *The process of education.* Cambridge, MA: Harvard University Press. NIH Publication No. 00-4769. Washington, DC: U.S. Department of Health and Human Services.

Bus, A. G., & van Ijzendoorn, M. H. (1999). Phonological awareness and early reading: A meta-analysis of experimental training studies. *Journal of Educational Psychology, 91*(3), 403–414.

Carnine, D., Silbert, J., Kame'enui, E. J., & Tarver, S. G. (2004). *Direct instruction reading* (4th ed.). Upper Saddle River, NJ: Pearson Prentice Hall.

Center for the Improvement of Early Reading Achievement (CIERA). (2001, May). *Constructing achievement orientations toward literacy: An analysis of sociocultural activity in Latino home and community contexts.* (CIERA Report #1–011). Retrieved July 20, 2007 from www.nifl.gov/partnershipforreading/publications/Cierra.pdf.

Center for the Improvement of Early Reading Achievement (CIERA). (2003). *Putting reading first: The research building blocks for teaching children to read*. Retrieved July 20, 2007, from www.nifl.gov/partnershipforreading/publications/Cierra.pdf.

Chall, J. S. (1967). *Learning to read: The great debate*. New York: McGraw-Hill.

Chall, J. S. (1983). *Literacy: Trends and explanations*. (ERIC Document Reproduction Service No. ED232135).

Chall, J. S. (1992). The new reading debates: Evidence from science, art, and ideology. *Teachers College Record, 94*(2), 315–328.

Chard, D., Vaughn, S., & Tyler, B. (2002). A synthesis of research on effective interventions for building reading fluency with elementary students with learning disabilities. *Journal of Learning Disabilities, 35*, 386–406.

Chiappe, P., Siegel, L. S., & Gottardo, A. (2002). Reading-related skills of kindergartners from diverse linguistic backgrounds. *Applied Psycholinguistics, 23*, 95–116.

Chiappe, P., Siegel, L. S., & Wade-Wooley, L. (2002). Linguistic diversity and the development of reading skills: A longitudinal study. *Scientific Studies of Reading, 6*(4), 369–400.

Christensen, C. A. (1997). Onset, rhymes, and phonemes in learning to read. *Scientific Studies of Reading, 1*, 341–358.

Cisero, C. A., & Royer, J. M. (1995). The development and cross-language transfer of phonological awareness. *Contemporary Educational Psychology, 20*, 275–303.

Clark, F. L. (2000). The strategies instruction model: A research-validated intervention for students with learning disabilities. *Learning Disabilities: A Multidisciplinary Journal, 10*, 209–217.

Clay, M. M. (1991). Introducing a new storybook to young readers. *Reading Teacher, 45*(4) 264–272.

Cole, A. D. (2006). Scaffolding beginning readers: Micro and macro cues teachers use during oral reading. *Reading Teacher, 59*(5), 450–459.

Coyne, M. D., Kame'enui, E. J., & Simmons, D. C. (2004). Teaching vocabulary during shared storybook readings: An examination of differential effects. *Exceptionality, 12*(3), 145–162.

Coyne, M. D., Kame'enui, E. J., Simmons, D. C., & Harn, B. (2004). Beginning reading intervention as inoculation or insulin: First-grade reading performance of strong responders to kindergarten intervention. *Journal of Learning Disabilities, 37*(2), 90–104.

Coyne, M. D., McCoach, D. B., & Kapp, S. (2007). Vocabulary intervention for kindergarten students: Comparing extended instruction to embedded instruction and incidental exposure. *Learning Disability Quarterly, 30*(2), 74–88.

Cummins, J. (1996). *Negotiating identities: Education for empowerment in a diverse society*. Ontario: California Association for Bilingual Education.

Cunningham, P. M. (2004). *Phonics they use*. Boston: Allyn & Bacon.

Cunningham, P. M., & Hall, D. P. (2001). *Making words*. Grand Rapids, MI: Schaffer.

Danne, M. C., Campbell, J. R., Grigg, W. S., Goodman, M. J., & Oranje, A. (2005). *Fourth-grade students reading aloud: NAEP 2002 Special Study of Oral Reading*.

Defior, S., & Tuydela, P. (1994). Effect of phonological training on reading and writing acquisition. *Reading and Writing: An Interdisciplinary Journal, 6*, 299–320.

Deno, S. L. (1985). Curriculum-based measurement: The emerging alternative. *Exceptional Children, 52*(3), 219–232.

Deno, S. L. (1986). Formative evaluation of individual student programs: A new role for school psychologists. *School Psychology Review, 15*, 358–374.

Deno, S. L. (2003). Developments in curriculum-based measurement. *Journal of Special Education, 37*, 184–192.

Denton, C. A. (2000). *The efficacy of two English reading interventions in a bilingual education program*. Unpublished doctoral dissertation, Texas A&M University.

Denton, C. A., Anthony, J. L., Parker, R., & Hasbrouck, J. E. (2006). Effects of two tutoring programs on the English reading development of Spanish-English bilingual students. *Elementary School Journal, 104*(4), 289–305.

Deshler, D. D., Schumaker, J., Bulgren, J., Lenz, K., Jantzen, J. E., Adams, G., Carnine, D., Grossen, B., Davis, B., & Marquis, J. (2001). Making learning easier: Connecting new knowledge to things students already know. *Teaching Exceptional Children, 33*(4), 82–85.

Donovan, S., & Cross, C. (2002). *Minority students in special and gifted education.* Washington, DC: National Academy Press.

Durgunoğlu, A.Y. (1998). Acquiring literacy in English and Spanish in the United States. In A.Y. Durgunoğlu & L. Verhoeven (Eds.), *Literacy development in a multilingual context: Cross-cultural perspectives* (pp. 135–146). Mahwah, NJ: Erlbaum.

Durgunoğlu, A. (2002). Cross-linguistic transfer in literacy development and implications for language learners. *Annals of Dyslexia, 52,* 189.

Durgunoğlu, A. Y., Nagy, W. E., & Hancin-Bhatt, B. J. (1993). Cross-language transfer of phonological awareness. *Journal of Educational Psychology, 85,* 453–465.

Durgunoğlu, A. Y., & Oeney, B. (1999). A cross-linguistic comparison of phonological awareness and word recognition. *Reading & Writing, 11*(4), 281–299.

Ehri, L. C., Nunes, S. R., Stahl, S. A., & Willows, D. M. (2001). Systematic phonics instruction helps students learn to read: Evidence from the National Reading Panel's meta-analysis. *Review of Educational Research, 71*(3), 393–447.

Ehri, L. C., Nunes, S. R., Willows, D. M., Schuster, B. V., Yaghoub-Zadeh, Z., & Shanahan, T. (2001). Phonemic awareness instruction helps children learn to read: Evidence from the National Reading Panel's meta-analysis. *Reading Research Quarterly, 36,* 250–287.

Elbaum, B., Vaughn, S., & Hughes, M. (1999). Grouping practices and reading outcomes for students with disabilities. *Exceptional Children, 65*(3), 399–415.

Engelmann, S. (1999). The benefits of direct instruction: Affirmative action for at-risk students. *Educational Leadership, 57,* 77–79.

Engelmann, S., Becker, W. C., Carnine, D. W., & Gersten, R. (1988) The direct instruction follow through model: Design and outcomes. *Education and Treatment of Children, 11*(4), 303–317.

Engelmann, S., & Bruner, E. C. (1997). *Reading mastery.* Chicago: Science Research Associates.

Engelmann, S., & Carnine, D. W. (1982). *Theory of instruction: Principles and applications.* Oregon: ADI Press.

Engelmann, S., Hanner, S., & Haddox, P. (1980). *Corrective reading.* Chicago: Science Research Associates.

Feldman, K. (2006). Helping older kids who struggle with reading. Retrieved from www.schwablearning.org/pdfs/expert_feldman.pdf?date=12–11–03.

Filippini, A. L. (2008). Effects of a vocabulary-added instructional intervention for at-risk English learners: Is efficient reading instruction more effective? Doctoral dissertation, University of California, Santa Barbara, 2008. *Dissertation Abstracts International, 68*(7-A), 2878.

Fletcher, J. M., Lyons, G. R., Fuchs, L. S., & Barnes, M. A. (2007). *Learning disabilities: From identification to intervention.* New York: Guilford Press.

Foorman, B., Francis, D., Winikates, D., Mehta, P., Schatschneider, C., & Fletcher, J. (1997). Early interventions for children with reading disabilities. *Scientific Studies of Reading, 1*(3), 255–276.

Friend, M. (2008). *Special education: Contemporary perspectives for school professionals.* Boston: Pearson Education.

Friend, M., & Bursuck, W. D. (2006). *Including students with special needs: A practical guide for classroom teachers* (4th ed.). Boston: Allyn & Bacon.

Fuchs, D., Fuchs, L. S., Mathes, P. G., & Simmons, D. C. (1997). Peer-assisted learning strategies: Making classrooms more responsive to academic diversity. *American Educational Research Journal, 34,* 174–206.

Fuchs, L. S., & Fuchs, D. (2007). The role of assessment in the three-tier approach to reading instruction. In D. Haager, J. K. Klingner & S. Vaughn (Eds.), *Evidence-based reading practices for response to intervention* (pp. 29–42). Baltimore: Brookes.

Fuchs, L. S., Fuchs, D., & Hamlett, C. L. (1993). Formative evaluation of academic progress: How much growth can we expect? *School Psychology Review, 22*(1), 27–48.

Fuchs, L. S., Fuchs, D., & Hollenbeck, K. N. (2007). Extending responsiveness to intervention to mathematics at first and third grades. *Learning Disabilities Research & Practice, 22*(1), 13–24.

Genesee, F., Geva, E., Dressler, C., & Kamil, M. L. (2006). Synthesis: Cross-linguistic relationship. In D. August & T. Shanahan (Eds.), *Developing literacy in second-language learners: Report of the National Literacy Panel on Language—minority children and youth.* Mahwah, NJ: Erlbaum.

Genesee, F., Linolm-Leary, K., Saunders, W. M., & Christian, D. (2006). *Educating language learners: A synthesis of research evidence.* New York: Cambridge University Press.

Genesee, F., Paradis, J., & Crago, M. B. (2006). *Dual language development and disorders.* Baltimore: Brookes.

Gerber, M., Jimenez, T., Leafstedt, J., Villaruz, J., Richards, C., & English, J. (2004). English reading effects of small-group intensive intervention in Spanish for K–1 English learners. *Learning Disabilities Research and Practice, 19*(4), 239–251.

Gersten, R., Baker, S. K., Shanahan, T., Linan-Thompson, S., Collins, P., & Scarcella, R. (2007). *Effective literacy and English language instruction for ELs in the elementary grades: A practice guide.* (NCEE no. 2007-4011). Washington, DC: National Center for Education Evaluation and Regional Assistance, Institute of Education Sciences, U.S. Department of Education. Available online at http://ies.ed.gov/ncee.

Gersten, R., Beaker, W. C., Heiry, T. J., & White, W. A. (1984). Entry IQ and yearly academic growth of children in direct instruction programs: A longitudinal study of low socioeconomic children. *Educational Evaluation and Policy Analysis, 6,* 109–121.

Gersten, R., Carnine, D., & Woodward, J. (1987). Direct instruction research: The third decade. *Remedial and Special Education, 8*(6), 48–56.

Gersten, R., & Geva, E. (2003). Teaching reading to early language learners. *Educational Leadership, 60,* 44–49.

Goldenberg, C., Rueda, R., & August, D. (2006). Synthesis: Sociocultural contexts and literacy development. In D. August & T. Shanahan (Eds.), *Report of the National Literacy Panel on Language—minority children and youth.* Mahwah, NJ: Erlbaum.

Good, R. H., & Kaminski, R. A. (Eds.). (2002). *Dynamic indicators of basic early literacy skills* (6th ed.). Eugene, OR: Institute for the Development of Education Achievement. Available online at http://dibels.uoregon.edu/.

Graves, M. F., Brunetti, G. J., & Slater, W. H. (1982). The reading vocabularies of primary grade children of varying geographic and social backgrounds. In J. A. Harris & L. A. Harris (Eds.), *New inquiries in reading research and instruction* (pp. 99–104). Rochester, NY: National Reading Conference.

Gunn, B., Biglan, A., Smolkowski, K., & Ary, D. (2000). The efficacy of supplemental instruction in decoding skills for Hispanic and non-Hispanic students in early elementary school. *Journal of Special Education, 34*(2), 90–103.

Haager, D., Calhoon, M. B., & Linan-Thompson, S. (2007). English language learners and response to intervention: Introduction to special issue. *Learning Disability Quarterly, 30,* 151–152.

Haager, D., Dimino, J. A., & Windmueller, M. P. (2007). *Interventions for reading success.* Baltimore: Brookes.

Haager, D., & Klingner, J. (2005). *Differentiated instruction in inclusive classrooms: The special educator's guide.* Boston: Allyn & Bacon.

Haager, D., Klingner, J. K., & Vaughn, S. (2007) *Evidence-based reading practices for response to intervention.* Baltimore: Brookes.

Hammill, D. D., & Swanson, H. L. (2006). The National Reading Panel's Meta-Analysis of Phonics Instruction: Another point of view. *Elementary School Journal, 107*(1), *Special issue: Reading lessons and federal policy making: An overview and introduction,* 17–26.

Hart, B., & Risley, T. R. (1995). *Meaningful differences in the everyday experience of young American children.* Baltimore: Brookes.

Hart, B., & Risley, T. R. (2003). The early catastrophe: The 30 million word gap by age 3. *American Educator, 27,* 4–9.

Heubusch, J., & Lloyd, J. L. (1998). Corrective feedback in oral reading. *Journal of Behavioral Education, 8*(1), 63–79.

Hiebert, E. H., Martin, L. A., & Menon, S. (2005). Are there alternatives in reading textbooks? An examination of three beginning reading programs. *Reading Writing Quarterly, 21,* 7–32.

Individuals with Disabilities Education Act of 1997, 20 U.S.C. § 1400 et seq. (amended 2004); 34 C.F.R. §§ 300.1 et seq. (2003).

Individuals with Disabilities Education Improvement Act of 2004, P. L. No. 108-446, 118 Stat. 2647 (2004) (amended 20 U.S.C. §§ 1400 et seq.).

Jiménez, T. (2004). Lexical restructuring: How the primary language impacts English reading development in ELs. Unpublished doctoral dissertation, University of California, Santa Barbara.

Jiménez, T. C., Filippini, A., & Gerber, M. (2006). Increasing children's oral language skills through primary language joint storybook reading. *Bilingual Research Journal, 30*(2), 431–452.

Jiménez, T. C., Graf., V. L., & Rose, E. (2007). Gaining access to general education: The promise of universal design for learning. *Issues in Teacher Education: Special Issue, 16*(2), 41–54.

Jongejan, W., Verhoeven, L., & Siegel, L. S. (2007). Predictors of reading and spelling abilities in first- and second-language learners. *Journal of Educational Psychology, 99*(4), 835–851.

Juel, C., Biancarosa, G., Coker, D., & Deffes, R. (2003). Walking with Rosie: A cautionary tale of early reading instruction. *Educational Leadership, 60,* 12–18.

Kavale, K. A., & Forness, S. R. (1987). Substance over style: Assessing the efficacy of modality testing and teaching. *Exceptional Children, 54*(3), 228–239.

Klingner, J. K., Artiles, A. J., & Barletta, L. M. (2006). English language learners who struggle with reading: Language acquisition or LD? *Journal of Learning Disabilities, 39*(2), 108–128.

Kohnert, K. (2008). *Language disorders in bilingual children and adults.* San Diego, CA: Plural Publishing.

Kouri, T. A., Selle, C. A., & Riley, S. A. (2006). Comparison of meaning and graphophonemic feedback strategies for guided reading instruction of children with language delays. *American Journal of Speech-Language Pathology, 15,* 236–246.

Krashen, S. (1996). A gradual exit, variable threshold model for limited-English-proficient children. *NABE News, 19*(7), 1, 15–17.

Leafstedt, J. M. (2003). Crossover of phonological processing skills: A study of Spanish-speaking students in two instructional settings. *Dissertation Abstracts International, 63*(10-A), 3473.

Leafstedt, J. M., & Gerber, M. M. (2005). Crossover of phonological processing skills: A study of Spanish speaking students in two instructional settings. *Remedial and Special Education, 26*(4), 226–235.

Leafstedt, J. M., Richards, C., & Gerber, M. (2004). Effectiveness of explicit phonological-awareness instruction for at-risk English learners. *Learning Disabilities Research and Practice, 19*(4), 252–261.

Lesaux, N., & Siegel, L. S. (2003). The development of reading in children who speak English as a second language. *Developmental Psychology, 39*(6), 1005–1019.

Limbos, M., & Geva, E. (2001). Accuracy of teacher assessments of ESL children at-risk for reading disability. *Journal of Learning Disabilities, 34,* 136–151.

Linan-Thompson, S., Cirino, P. T., & Vaughn, S. (2007). Determining English language learners' response to intervention: Questions and some answers. *Learning Disability Quarterly, 30,* 185–195.

Linan-Thompson, S., Vaughn, S., Hickman-Davis, P., & Kouzekanani, K. (2003). Effectiveness of supplemental reading instruction for second-grade English language learners with reading difficulties. *Elementary School Journal, 103*(3), 221–238.

Linan-Thompson, S., Vaughn, S., Prater, K., & Cirino, P. T. (2006). The response to intervention of English language learners at risk for reading problems. *Journal of Learning Disabilities 39*(5), 390–398.

Lloyd, J. (1984). How shall we individualize instruction—or should we? *Remedial and Special Education, 5,* 7–15.

MacMillan, D., & Siperstein, G. (2002). Learning disabilities as operationally defined by schools. In R. Bradley, L. Danielson, & D. Hallahan (Eds), *Identification of learning disabilities: Research to practice* (pp. 287–333). Mahwah, NJ: Erlbaum.

Malloy, K. J., Gilbertson, D., & Maxfield, J. (2007). Research into practice: Use of brief experimental analysis for selecting reading interventions for English language learners. *School Psychology Review, 36*(2), 291–310.

Marriot, D. (1997). *What are the other kids doing while you teach small groups?* Huntington Beach, CA: Creative Teaching Press.

McDonnell, S. A., Friel-Patti, S., & Rollins, P. R. (2003). Patterns of change in maternal-child discourse behaviors across repeated storybook readings. *Applied Psycholinguistics, 24,* 323–341.

Menzies, H., & Falvey, M. (2008). Inclusion of students with disabilities in general education. In T. C. Jimenez & V. Graf (Eds.), *Education for all: Critical issues in the education of children and youth with disabilities* (pp. 71–100). San Francisco: Jossey-Bass.

Nagy, W. E., Herman, P. A., & Anderson, R. C. (1985). Learning words from context. *Reading Research Quarterly, 20*(2), 233–253.

National Assessment of Educational Progress. (2002). Oral reading study. Retrieved August 2008 from http://nces.ed.gov/nationsreportcard/studies/ors/.

National Institute of Child Health and Human Development. (2000). *Report of the National Reading Panel. Teaching children to read: An evidence-based assessment of the scientific research literature on reading and its implications for reading instruction* (NIH Publication No. 00-4769). Washington, DC: U.S. Government Printing Office.

National Reading Panel (NRP). (2000). *Teaching children to read: An evidence-based assessment of the scientific research literature on reading and its implications for reading instruction* (NIH Publication No. 00-4769). Washington, DC: U.S. Department of Health and Human Services.

Nelson, J. S., Alber, S. R., & Gordy, A. (2004). Effects of systematic error correction and repeated readings on the reading accuracy and proficiency of second graders with disabilities. *Education and Treatment of Children, 27*(3), 186–198.

No Child Left Behind Act of 2001, P. L. No. 107–110, 20 U.S.C. 6301 et seq.

O'Connor, R. E. (2007). Layers of intervention that affect outcomes in reading. In D. Haager, J. Klingner & S. Vaughn (Eds.), *Evidence-based reading practices for response to intervention* (pp. 139–157). Baltimore: Brookes.

Palinscar, A. S., & Brown, A. L. (1984). Reciprocal teaching: Activities to promote reading with your mind. In T. L. Harris & E. J. Cooper (Eds.), *Reading, thinking and concept development: Strategies for the classroom.* New York: College Board.

Penno, J. F., Wilkinson, I. A. G., & Moore, D. W. (2002). Vocabulary acquisition from teacher explanation and repeated listening to stories: Do they overcome the Matthew effect? *Journal of Educational Psychology, 94*(1), 23–33.

Porche, M. V. (2001). Parent involvement as a link between home and school. In D. K. Dickinson & P. O. Tabors (Eds.), *Beginning literacy with language* (pp. 291–312). Baltimore: Brookes.

Pressley, M., El-Dinary, P. B., Gaskins, I., Schuder, T., Bergman, J., Almasi, L., & Brown, R. (1992). Beyond direct explanation: Transactional instruction of reading comprehension strategies. *Elementary School Journal, 92,* 511–554.

Richards, C., Leafstedt, J. M., & Gerber, M. M. (2006). Qualitative and quantitative examination of four low-performing kindergarten English learners: Characteristics of responsive and nonresponsive students. *Remedial and Special Education, 27*(4), 218–234.

Robbins, C., & Ehri, L. C. (1994). Reading storybooks to kindergarteners helps them to learn new vocabulary words. *Journal of Educational Psychology, 86,* 54–64.

Schatschneider, C., Fletcher, J. M., Francis, D. J., Carlson, C. D., & Foorman, B. R. (2004). Kindergarten prediction of reading skills: A longitudinal comparative analysis. *Journal of Educational Psychology, 96*(2), 265–282.

Shanahan, T., & Beck, I. L. (2006). Effective literacy teaching for English-language learners. In D. August & T. Shanahan (Eds.), *Developing literacy in second language learners: Report of the National Literacy Panel on Language—minority children and youth* (pp. 445–488). Mahwah, NJ: Erlbaum.

Shinn, M. R., Shinn, M. M., Hamilton, C., & Clarke, B. (2002). Using curriculum-based measurement in general education classrooms to promote reading success. In M. Shinn, H. M. Hill & G. Stoner (Eds.), *Interventions for academic and behavior problems II: Preventive and remedial approaches* (pp. 113–142). Bethesda, MD: NASP Publications.

Simmons, D. C., & Kame'enui, E. J. (1998). *What reading research tells us about children with diverse learning needs: Bases and basics.* Mahwah, NJ: Erlbaum.

Smith, D. D. (2004). *Introduction to special education: Teaching in an age of opportunity*. Boston, MA: Allyn & Bacon.

Snow, C. E., Burns, M. S., & Griffin, P. (Eds.). (1998). *Preventing reading difficulties in young children*. Washington, DC: National Research Council, National Academy Press.

Solari, E. J., & Gerber, M. M. (2008). Early comprehension instruction for Spanish-speaking English language learners: Teaching text level reading skills while maintaining effects on word level skills. *Learning Disabilities Research and Practice, 23*, 155–169.

Solari, E. J., & Richards, C. (2008). Responsiveness in EL populations: Student variables. Paper presented at the Pacific Coast Research Conference, Coronado, CA.

Speece, D. L., & Walker, C. Y. (2007). What are the issues in response to intervention research? In D. Haager, J. K. Klingner & S. Vaughn (Eds.), *Evidence-based reading practices for response to intervention* (pp. 287–301). Baltimore: Brookes.

Stanovich, K. E. (1986). Matthew effects in reading: Some consequences of individual differences in the acquisition of literacy. *Reading Research Quarterly, 21*(4), 360–406.

Stanovich, K. E., & Siegel, L. S. (1994). Phenotypic performance profile of children with reading disabilities: A regression-based tests of the phonological-core variable-difference model. *Journal of Educational Psychology, 86*(1), 24–53.

Stuebing, K. K., Fletcher, J. M., LeDoux, J. M., Lyon, R. G., Shaywitz, S. E., & Shaywitz, B. A. (2002). Validity of IQ discrepancy classifications of reading disabilities: A meta-analysis. *Annals of Dyslexia, 39*(2), 469–518.

Swanson, H. L., & Hoskyn, M. (1998). Experimental intervention research on students with learning disabilities: A meta-analysis of treatment outcomes. *Review of Educational Research, 68*, 277–321.

Teachers of English to Speakers of Other Languages (TESOL). (2007). Individual differences and educational backgrounds. Retrieved March 2008 from www.tesol.org/s_tesol/sec_tapestry.asp?CID=1585&DID=8857 <http://www.tesol.org/s_tesol/sec_tapestry.asp?CID=1585&DID=8857>

Torgesen, J. K. (1999). Phonologically based reading disabilities: Toward a coherent theory of one kind of learning disability. In R. J. Sternberg & L. Spear-Swerling (Eds.), *Perspectives on learning disabilities* (pp. 321–362). New Haven, CT: Westview Press.

Torgesen, J. K. (2000). Individual differences in response to early interventions in reading: The lingering problem of treatment resisters. *Learning Disabilities Research and Practice, 15*(1), 55–64.

Torgesen, J. K., Alexander, A. W., Wagner, R. K., Rashotte, C. A., Voeller, K. K., & Conway, T. (2001). Intensive remedial instruction for children with severe reading disabilities: Immediate and long-term outcomes from two instructional approaches. *Journal of Learning Disabilities, 34*, 33–58.

Torgesen, J. K., & Davis, C. (1996). Individual difference variables that predict response to training in phonological awareness. *Journal of Experimental Child Psychology, 63*(1), 1–21.

Torgesen, J. K., Wagner, R. K., & Rashotte, C. A. (1999). Preventing reading failure in young children with phonological processing disabilities: Group and individual responses to instruction. *Journal of Educational Psychology, 91*(4), 579–593.

U.S. Department of Education & National Insititute of Child Health and Human Development. (2003). *National symposium on learning disabilities in English language learners. Symposium summary*. Washington, DC: Authors.

Van Hook, J., & Fix, M. (2000). A profile of immigrant students in U.S. schools. In J. Ruiz-de-Velasco and M. Fix (Eds), *Overlooked and underserved: Immigrant students in U.S. secondary schools* (pp. 9–33). Washington, DC: Urban Institute.

Vaughn, S., Cirino, P. T., Linan-Thompson, S., Mathes, P. G., Carlson, C. D., Cardenas Hagan, E., et al. (2006). Effectiveness of a Spanish intervention and an English intervention for English-language learners at risk for reading problems. *American Educational Research Journal, 43*(3), 449–487.

Vaughn, S., Gersten, R., & Chard, D. J. (2000). The underlying message in LD intervention research: Findings from research syntheses. *Exceptional Children, 67*, 99–114.

Vaughn, S., & Klingner, J. K. (2007). Overview of the three-tier model of reading intervention. In D. Haager, J. K. Klingner & S. Vaughn (Eds.), *Evidence-based reading practices for response to intervention* (pp. 3–9). Baltimore: Brookes.

Vaughn, S., Linan-Thompson, S., & Hickman, P. (2003). Response to intervention as a means of identifying students with reading/learning disabilities. *Exceptional Children, 69*, 391–410.

Vaughn, S., Linan-Thompson, S., Mathes, P. G., Cirino, P. T., Carlson, C. D., Pollard-Durodola, S. D., Cardenas-Hagan, E., & Francis, D. J. (2006). Effectiveness of Spanish intervention for first-grade English language learners at risk for reading difficulties. *Journal of Learning Disabilities, 39*(1), 56–73.

Vaughn, S., Mathes, P. G., Linan-Thompson, S., & Francis, D. J. (2005). Teaching English language learners at-risk for reading disabilities to read: Putting research into practice. *Learning Disabilities: Research & Practice, 20*(1), 58–67.

Vaughn, S., & Roberts, G. (2007). Secondary interventions in reading: Providing additional instruction for students at-risk. *Teaching Exceptional Children, 39*, 40–46.

Vaughn, S., Wanzek, J., Woodruff, A., & Linan-Thompson, S. (2007). Prevention and early identification of students with reading disabilities. In D. Haager, J. Klingner, & S. Vaughn (Eds.), *Evidence-based reading practices for response to intervention* (pp. 11–27). Baltimore: Brookes.

Villa, R., Thousand, J., & Nevin, A. (2004). *A guide to co-teaching: Practical tips for facilitating student learning.* Thousand Oaks, CA: Corwin Press.

Vygotsky, L. S. (1962). *Thought and language.* Cambridge, MA: MIT Press.

Wagner, R. K., & Torgesen, J. K. (1987). The nature of phonological processing and its causal role in the acquisition of reading skills. *Psychological Bulletin, 101*(2), 192–212

Wagner, R., Torgeson, J. K., & Rashotte, C. A. (1994, January 1). Development of reading-related phonological processing abilities: New evidence of bidirectional causality from a latent variable longitudinal study. *Developmental Psychology, 30*(1), 73–87.

Wagner, R. K., & Torgeson, J. K, Rashotte, C. A., Hecht, S., Barker, T., & Burgess, S. (1997). Changing causal relations between phonological processing abilities and word-level reading as children develop from beginning readers to fluent readers: A five year longitudinal study. *Developmental Psychology, 33*, 486–479.

Wallace, T., Espin, C. A., McMaster, K., Deno, S. L., & Foegen, A. (2007). CBM progress monitoring within a standards-based system. *Journal of Special Education, 41*(2), 66–67.

Wayman, M. M., Wallace, T., & Wiley, H. I. (2007). Literature synthesis on curriculum-based measurement in reading. *Journal of Special Education, 41*(2), 85–120.

White, T. G., Graves, M. F., & Slater, W. H. (1990). Growth of reading vocabulary in diverse elementary schools: Decoding and word meaning. *Journal of Educational Psychology, 82*(2), 281–290.

White, W. A. T. (1988). A meta-analysis of the effects of direct instruction in special education. *Education and Treatment of Children, 11*(4), 364–374.

Windmueller, M. P. (2004). *Early reading predictors of literacy achievement for English learners: A longitudinal study from first through third grade.* Doctoral dissertation, University of Southern California, 2004. *Dissertation Abstracts International, 65*, 25–43.

Wolery, M., & Gast, D. L. (1984). Effective and efficient procedures for the transfer of stimulus control. *Topics in Early Childhood Special Education, 4*(3), 52–77.

Index

Note: Page numbers followed by letters *b, f,* and *t* refer to boxes, figures, and tables, respectively.

Decoding, 19, 78
and comprehension, 23
daily practice in, 42
and fluency, 24f, 25
progress monitoring for, 53,
53f, 55f
students with learning
disabilities and, 60
Developmental Reading
Assessment (DRA), 57, 123
DI. *See* Direct instruction
DIBELS. *See* Dynamic Indicators
of Basic Early Literacy Skills
Direct instruction (DI), 61–63
Core Intervention Model
compared with, 92, 107
and corrective feedback,
62–63
Discrepancy model of learning
disabilities, 8, 48
response to intervention as
alternative to, 69
DISTAR program, 20
DRA. *See* Developmental Reading
Assessment
Dynamic Indicators of Basic Early
Literacy Skills (DIBELS), 5,
51, 117b
benchmarks for measuring
growth, 129
data provided in, 119, 120t
and progress monitoring, 51,
52t, 54t, 56

Early reading
definition of, 25–26
trajectory for growth in, 26,
27f
Early reading intervention
activities for students not
included in, 143–144
breakdown of skills in, 97–98,
99f
components of reading
included in, 76–77
content and materials selected
for, 95–96, 96t, 143t, 145

corrective feedback in, 62–63,
102–107, 103f
data-based decision making
before, 113f, 114–127
data-based decision making
during, 127–134, 128f
data-based decision making
after, 134–139, 135f
designing, 121–124, 125t, 126t,
138–139
direct instruction in, 61–62
for English learners, 31, 38–42
explicit instruction in, 97–98
first two weeks of, 124, 125t,
126t, 127
vs. general classroom
instruction, 9–11, 10t, 27–28
goals of, 94–95, 94t, 121–123
implementing, 142–147, 143t
individual differences guiding,
5–6, 11
intensive, 98–100
length and frequency of, 10,
93b, 134
making time for, 142–143
maximizing student responses
in, 100–102, 101b
modeling in, 85, 97
modifying, based on data, 132,
133
response to intervention model
and, 7–8, 8t
in small groups, 93–94, 98
strategy instruction in, 64
for students with learning
disabilities, 59–66
success of, 26, 27f
Early Reading Project, 4
Early Reading Project
Intervention (ERPI), 4
development of, 4–5
response to intervention model
and, 9
scope and sequence of, 5,
81–90, 82t
Echo reading, with English
learners, 43t

Effective Literacy and English
Language Instruction for ELs
in the Elementary Grades
(report), 39
English learners (ELs), 30–46
assessment of, 114–115, 116b
and comprehension, 37, 116b
and context-reduced materials,
37
and cross-linguistic transfer,
33, 40, 79
early reading intervention for,
31, 38–42
factors affecting language and
literacy outcomes, 32
fluency interventions for,
41–42, 116b
grouping for intervention, 39,
43t, 119
home-school connections for,
44t, 45
individual differences among,
32–38
vs. learning disabilities, 30–31,
34–35, 36t
oral English proficiency
among, 35
phonics interventions for, 41,
79, 89–90, 115
and phonological awareness,
33–34, 114
phonological awareness
interventions for, 40–41, 79,
85–86
poor academic outcomes for,
30
response to intervention
among, 31
supplemental instruction to
support, 43–45, 43t, 44t
and vocabulary development,
37, 39
vocabulary interventions for,
42, 43t
ERPI. *See* Early Reading Project
Intervention
Error analysis, 129

Evidence-based reading instruction, 7
Explicit instruction, 97–98
Expository text, comprehension strategies for, 22

Family outreach, 44t, 45
Feedback. *See* Corrective feedback
Flashcards, using with ELs, 41, 43t
Fluency, 17t, 20–21
  and comprehension, 21, 23, 24, 24f, 25
  curriculum-based measurement of, 128
  decoding and, 24f, 25
  English learners and, 41–42, 116b
  growth rates for, 129
  progress-monitoring data on, 133f
  students with learning disabilities and, 60
Follow Through (study), 20

General classroom instruction, 11, 15
  vs. intervention, 9–11, 10t, 27–28
  students with learning disabilities and, 58, 59, 65–66
Goals
  in Core Intervention Model, 94–95, 94t
  of Individual Education Program (IEP), 63–64, 69
  of intervention, determining, 121–123, 145
  in second session of intervention, 138, 139
Graphs, progress-monitoring, 53, 53f, 55f, 147
Groups/grouping, intervention, 5–6
  data-based decision making and, 119–121, 120t, 121t

English learners and, 39, 43t, 119
planning for, 124
progress-monitoring data and changes in, 132, 132t
second round of, 137, 138t
size of, 93–94, 98
students with learning disabilities and, 65, 121
weekly record of, 56
Growth
  assessment after intervention, 134, 137, 144, 151
  benchmarks for measuring, 129
  in first-grade reading, 26, 27f
  student responses and, 101b
Guided practice, 98, 99f

Home literacy activities, 44t, 45

IDEIA. *See* Individuals with Disabilities Education Improvement Act
IEP. *See* Individual Education Program
Imitation, in staircase correction model, 103, 105
Independent practice, 98, 99f
Independent working time, for students not in intervention, 143
Individual differences
  content and materials guided by, 95, 96f
  among English learners, 32–38
  intervention guided by, 5–6, 11
  in learning to read, 14–16
  among struggling readers, 119, 120t
Individual Education Program (IEP)
  and discrepancy model of learning disability, 48
  goals and objectives of, 63–64, 69
  and intervention planning, 124

Individual responses, maximizing, 100–102
Individuals with Disabilities Education Improvement Act (IDEIA), 7, 31, 69
Information-processing theory, and staircase approach, 105
Instruction. *See also* General classroom instruction
  explicit, 97–98
  vs. intervention, 9–11, 10t, 27–28
  modifying based on data, 132, 133
Instructional reading level, 123, 138–139
Intensive intervention, 98–100
Interactive writing assignments, 65–66
Intervention. *See also* Early reading intervention; Phonics; Phonological awareness
  vs. instruction, 9–11, 10t, 27–28
  intensive, 98–100
Intervention groups. *See* Groups/grouping
Interventions for Reading Success (Haager et al.), 145

Language level, grouping by, 119
Learning center, 68t, 73
Learning disabilities. *See also* Special education
  and access to core reading and language arts instruction, 65–66
  assessment of, 115–118, 117b
  and continuous review, 98
  and corrective feedback, 62–63
  designing intervention for, 123, 124, 138–139
  and direct instruction, 61–62
  discrepancy model of, 8, 48, 49–50